Easy Ayurveda

Recipes &

Cookbook

Recipes for Weight Loss, Hormonal
Balance, Heart Health, Pregnancy, Old
Age & Mental Well-Being

I0491637

By

Lakshmi Vemuri

*Copyright © 2021 – **CSBA Publishing House***

All Rights Reserved.

Published by:

CSBA
PUBLISHING HOUSE

CSBA Publishing House

Cover & Interior designed

By

Cindy Roberts

First Edition

Table of Content

Ayurvedic Recipes: Introduction

Ayurveda is science for some, a mystery for some, and an alternative healing system for some. And, I'd say Ayurveda is all of them. Or should I say, Ayurveda is a mysterious healing science?!

Well, it has been almost a decade since I've first started making use of this ancient medical system. Ever since that, my life has immensely got better. Over this decade-long journey, I've discovered so many amazing things about our food, body, and mind. And, I can safely say, I've overcome the mystery part of it. Here, I will extensively cover all the important aspects of this system, mainly focusing on peeling off the mystery layers surrounding it.

While incorporating Ayurveda into my lifestyle, I've realized that the tasty and healthy food it offers is my absolute favorite. Oh yeah, you can seamlessly have delicious and healthy food at the same, thanks to Ayurveda.

Oops, I've just now realized that I haven't really introduced myself. Alright! I'm Lakshmi, hailing from India. Yep! The land where Ayurveda has been found. I've suffered multiple ailments all through my childhood into my teen years. No allopathic medicine has helped me, at least to cure my health problems. It all changed when I got introduced to Ayurvedic food by none other than my maternal grandmother.

Since its inception, Ayurveda has become an integral part of our daily lives, through food, medicine, exercise, and many other things. However, sadly, the current generation has been growing away from this system. Only a few people like me are fondly interested in it.

I'm writing this book to educate people from all over the world about the benefits of Ayurvedic food. How am I going to do that?! Well, by providing about 100 recipes of super-tasty and immensely-healthy Ayurvedic food items.

If you have gained anything from this book, would you do me a favor? I would very much appreciate it if you could leave a review online where you purchased this book. Online reviews help my books reach more people.

Before going to the recipes part, I'd like to explain to you a bit about Ayurveda, its significance, the way it works, and a few other related things. So, without any further ado, let's begin.

What is Ayurveda?

Ayurveda is a complete holistic healing system that mainly focuses on offering a healthy lifestyle. Ayurveda believes in the infamous saying, 'Prevention is better than cure.' However, one can also use this system to heal or cure their existing ailments.

Experts say that Ayurveda was found 5,000 years ago in Ancient India and then spread across different parts of the world, especially Asia. Ayurveda is a combination of two words, Ayur=Life and Veda=Science of knowledge.

Ever since then, it has evolved into a comprehensive health system, suitable for almost all types of health issues.

Oh, Ayurveda can also be used to treat mental health issues, not only physical health problems.

Moreover, it's a lifestyle, when properly adapted to, can bring you joy and happiness into your life. Well, a healthy body and mind can hugely improve your life, don't you think so? Anyhow, here are a few interesting facts about Ayurveda:

Many people think that Ayurveda is all about plants and herbs. Oh no, it's a very bad misconception about this amazing holistic science. Ayurveda has all types of elements, which help you lead a healthy life. In Ayurveda, you're going to eat basic things such as ghee, honey, butter, and ghee, along with spices and herbs, to improve your life.

Ayurveda has different branches of medicinal systems such as Bhutavaidya (Psychiatry), Shalya-chikitsa (Surgery), Shalakya (treating health conditions above your shoulder area), Kaayachikitsa (Internal Medicine), Kaumarabhrutyam (Paediatrics), Agadatantram (Toxicology), and Rasayanam (Rejuvenation).

Ayurveda is very effective and can offer long-term health benefits when used properly. This science believes that the human body is made of 5 natural elements, which are Earth, Fire, Water, Space, and Air.

Ayurveda is so effective because it fights the cause of a disease rather than the symptoms. This is very important, as combating just the symptoms comes with the risk of repeated health issues.

Origins and History of Ayurveda

Honestly, no one knows the exact origin of Ayurveda. However, according to the popular belief in Indian, where this science has originated, a few thousand years ago, ancient Indian sages received the divine knowledge of Ayurveda and Yoga from the Hindu gods. From then on, the information has been passed onto the next generations.

Ayurveda is part of the Four Vedas, which are divine to the Indians. They are the oldest literature pieces that are still in existence. Vedas are written in the ancient Indian language, Sanskrit. The four Vedas are Sama Veda, Rig Veda, Atharva Veda, and Yajur Veda. Ayurveda is a part of the Atharva Veda.

Importance of Ayurveda

What can I say, about the importance of a millennia-old health system, that is too based on all-natural ingredients without any chemicals?! Well, Ayurveda has proven time and again that it's one of the most effective medical systems in the world.

Also, it incorporates several lifestyle elements such as diet, exercise, and meditation, to treat an illness. No fancy things here! Anyhow, to demonstrate the significance of Ayurveda, I'd like to tell you about some of the best health benefits it offers. After getting to know them, you be the judge and see how important it seems.

Health Benefits of Ayurvedic Food

Weight Loss

Ayurveda helps you with your weight-loss journey, that too, without the use of any chemicals or artificial substances. Moreover, it does this without impacting your emotional and physical stability. Ayurvedic food helps in detoxifying your body, purifying your skin, regulating your blood flow, and reducing excess amounts of cholesterol and fat.

Stress Buster

Ayurvedic food, when combined with Yoga workouts, can really help you in dealing with your stress, anxiety, and even depression. You don't have to swallow a bunch of pills every day to deal with such issues. Moreover, the Ayurvedic lifestyle encourages discipline, which also is very beneficial in maintaining a balanced and stress-less life.

Hormonal Balance

One of the main reasons for a lot of long-term and short-term ailments is hormonal imbalances. Whether it's your hair loss issue or your lack of enthusiasm in life, you can almost always find some hormonal imbalance in your life. Ayurveda again can save you here. Since it mainly focuses on detoxifying your body and providing crucial nutrients and vitamins, you can forget about imbalances in your hormone levels.

Reduced Inflammation

Either lack of proper sleep or poor diet is the main culprit if you're suffering from regular inflammation issues. Ayurvedic food, which consists of several medicinal herbs such as ashwagandha, turmeric, ginger, and Boswellia, not only detoxifies your body but also reduces inflammation. Boswellia, here, needs a special mention as it helps in treating arthritis, back pain, and bowel diseases. Ashwagandha, on the other hand, helps in developing tissues.

Eliminates Toxic Elements From Your Body

'Panchakarma,' a well-known Ayurvedic treatment method, helps in cleansing your body, mind, and soul. This treatment focuses on removing toxins from your body, which in-turn helps in the proper functioning of your body. The ayurvedic diet consists of several dishes and drinks that will aid you in detoxifying your entire body. In recent years, there has been a fad where the younger ones are obsessed with body detoxification, where they would spend hundreds or even thousands of dollars on useless products. Here, all they need is a proper Ayurvedic lifestyle.

Less Chances of Diseases

If you follow the Ayurvedic diet for at least 4-5 days a week, I can assure you that you can simply avoid any type of disease. I don't even remember the last time I got sick. Since Ayurveda works on preventing any ailments before they even attack your body, it's safe to say that you can stay healthy for a long time.

Healthy and Shiny Skin

As a woman, I prioritize my skin by a huge margin. After all, how can we, women, look beautiful when our skin is dry and pale?! In the last 5 years, I haven't used a single sunscreen or moisturizer product, thanks to Ayurvedic food. Moreover, not only the skin but my hair is also long, shiny, and healthy. Ayurvedic food comes with all the necessary natural ingredients to keep your skin and hair healthy.

Cures Insomnia

Every person, at some point in their lives, may have suffered from insomnia. I'd say it's difficult to avoid all your life. However, unfortunately, some people suffer from this issue all their lives, or for the majority of it. Ayurveda has several tips for you to avoid suffering from this disease. For example, having warm almond milk before bed can help you immensely in getting a night of good sleep.

Decreases Bloating

If you eat too much, you'll most probably suffer from bloating issues. You may also develop this issue if you have disturbed bowel movements. Bloating is usually caused by high levels of gas, which also causes pain, discomfort, and a stuffed abdomen. As Ayurvedic food is rich in spices and roots such as ginger, cardamom, and cumin, you can now treat your bloating issues easily. These ingredients also help in better digestion.

The Three Doshas

Before explaining about the Doshas, I'd like to talk about something first. See, there's a huge difference between the way Ayurveda works and the western medicine works. The allopathic systems focus on identifying the disease and its symptoms and then work on it. However, Ayurveda mainly focuses on the bodily energies and the balance between them.

According to Ayurveda, the bodily energies need to be in proper balance, which helps in developing a strong immune system. When your immune system is strong and balanced, your body takes care of all the diseases and fights them off.

Now, Ayurveda says that our body has three key energies, which are Vata, Pitta, and Kapha. And they are called Doshas. One must maintain a balance between these energies to lead a healthy life without any diseases and ailments. Some people contain one dominant dosha, where are some other people have two or even three dominant doshas. So, here are the three Doshas.

Vata

The Vata dosha provides the necessary energy required for all the body motions. It's extremely important and helps you stay balanced. Seasonally, Vata is highly active in the Fall and also active at the times of seasonal changes. These are times where you need to very careful about lifestyle and diet.

Since Vata dosha is predominantly the moving energy of your body, you need to give importance to your lifestyle and daily practices.

People who are Vata-dominant are blessed with flexibility, creativity, and a quick mind. They're usually psychologically sound and also are quick to grasp new concepts. However, these people are also prone to quickly forget the things they learn. So, meditation can help here. Vata people also walk, talk, and move very quickly. They also are easily-fatigued, thanks to their restless body movements.

Even though these people have high levels of intelligence, they also suffer from severe mental health issues such as anxiety, lack of confidence, intolerance, and several others. So, one must definitely focus on having a clear and healthy mindset. When Vata people are unbalanced, they feel anxious, nervous, and paranoid.

Vata people also have inconsistent digestion and appetite. They are usually attracted to foods like raw vegetables and salads. They also generate less urine, which may also cause several bladder-related health issues.

The Vata energy is mainly focused in the colon area, along with ears, brain, bones, skin, joints, and thighs. Vata people are mainly vulnerable to diseases such as pneumonia, emphysema, and arthritis. They may also suffer from some other common issues such as twitches, tics, aching joints, and nerve disorders. The Vata energy grows with age, which, if imbalanced, causes dry and wrinkled skin.

The qualities of Vata dosha are light, dry, cold, subtle, rough, mobile, and clear. So, any of such qualities, if in excess, can cause severe imbalances. Vata types must avoid taking excess alcohol, frequent travel, over-eating of sugars, and loud noises.

For Vata people, not only a good diet is enough, but they also must focus on having a good sleep, preferably going to bed by 10 PM.

Pitta

Pitta people can be compared to the element of fire. They have many similar qualities, such as sharp, agitating, penetrating, and hot. Pitta people usually have warm bodies, sharp intelligence, and penetrating ideas.

These people are very prone to becoming easily agitated

and are short-tempered, of course, only when the dosha is imbalanced. The Pitta people are, on average, medium-sized people, with average height and body. They also possess copper skin, freckles, and moles.

Their skin, however, is less-wrinkled when compared to Vata types. These people may experience premature greying of skin and hair. They are also prone to hair loss.

People are who are Pitta-dominant have a strong metabolism, strong appetite, and good digestion. They prefer cold drinks and hot spices. To balance this dosha, one must consider consuming sweet, astringent, and bitter-rich foods. Pitta people also enjoy sound sleep. They also produce urine in large quantities, which is good for their bladder.

Psychologically, Pitta people are highly intelligent, alert, and possess good memory power. They also can comprehend any subject with ease. However, when imbalanced, they experience emotions such as irrational anger, fear, and jealousy. They also love to flaunt their possessions and wealth.

Pitta people usually suffer from inflammatory diseases, regular fevers, and jaundice. Pitta people shouldn't consume too much liquid, spices, and hot foods. This dosha is highly active when the temperatures are hot. So, if you are a Pitta, try to have a special focus on your diet in the Summer.

Kapha

Kapha people are blessed with endurance, strength, and stamina. They also come with stable, grounded, and sweet temperaments. They usually have smooth and oily skin. Physically, these people can easily gain weight, leading to several health issues. They also have very slow metabolisms.

Kapha types mostly have thick skins, well-developed muscles, and bodies. People who are Kapha-dominant have large eyes, long lashes, and thick brows, which are usually attractive facial features.

Kapha people have poor bowel movements, making it slow and hard to evacuate. Their perspiration is moderate. However, they experience long and deep sleep. They're attracted to salty, oily, and sweet foods. To balance this dosha, you need to consume pungent, astringent, and bitter foods.

Mentally, Kapha types tend to be tolerant, forgiving, and calm. But they also tend to be lethargic, which makes it difficult for them to comprehend and grasp new things and concepts.

If you're a Kapha, you may fall sick to sinus, flu, and congestion issues. You may also be prone to diseases related to mucus. Kapha types are also sluggish, inclined to have diabetes, excess weight, and water retention issues.

Winter is the season where this dosha may become imbalanced. Not only in the winters but whenever there's a decline in the temperatures, you need to keep an eye on the diet and lifestyle. Working out regularly and keeping a check on your weight can benefit you and help you stay balanced. Moreover, if you're a Kapha, try to avoid excess consumption of sugars.

Ayurveda and Food

Ayurveda is all about food, right? Well, sorry, not so right, I have to say! Ayurveda is a complete health system with which you can lead a healthy life. However, food is one of the most important parts of Ayurveda.

Actually, I'd even go one step further and say that food is the most important element of this system. With a proper diet, you can avoid all types of diseases and have a healthy life both physically and mentally. Since this is primarily a recipe book, why not discuss a bit about the

Ayurvedic food?!

Food and its Importance in Ayurveda

Ayurveda believes in "Food is Medicine." Oh yeah, you can see how important the food is in Ayurveda, don't you?!

If you think about it, it really makes sense. A person living on pizzas and burgers is obviously going to get fat and unhealthy. On the other hand, a person who consumes plant-based food, fruits, and vegetables leads a happy and healthy life.

Now, tell me, isn't food a form of medicine?

The Ayurvedic diet propagates several food habits that are highly beneficial to your health. Here are a few things you need to learn about Ayurvedic food.

Promotes Consumption of Whole Foods

The Ayurvedic diet prescribes different diet plans for different doshas. However, among all the diets, one thing is common, which is the consumption of whole foods.

Eating whole foods such as vegetables, fruits, legumes, and grains can enhance your health by leaps and bounds. These foods are rich in minerals and nutrients, which are very necessary for a healthy body and mind alike.

An Ayurvedic diet also discourages processed food, which is not so good for your body. Since they lack fiber, they cause digestion problems, which, in turn, negatively affects several bodily functions.

Helps in Weight Loss

If you regularly consume a diet according to Ayurveda, you may relax and forget about excessive weight problems. Yes, you can avoid getting obese by eating Ayurvedic food.

Since this diet is completely natural and eliminates any type of junk and processed food items, the chances of getting overweight are slim to none. Also, if you're already overweight, you can shift to the Ayurvedic dietary habits and move forward in your weight loss journey seamlessly.

I, myself, had benefitted greatly from this diet since I used to be fat and unhealthy a few years ago. That's not the case anymore!

Promotes Mindfulness

In the current generation of hurry-burry lifestyles, which are overloaded with excess amounts of work-pressures, maintaining a healthy mind is extremely difficult.

As a result of that, people nowadays are easily developing several mental health issues. Ayurveda promotes mindfulness by suggesting natural and healthy foods. Along with that, Ayurveda also suggests you meditate for a few minutes before or after your meal.

By doing so, you're calming your mind, which in turn helps you keep mental health issues at bay. Consuming leafy vegetables regularly can also greatly help your mind and soul. Since Ayurvedic diet focuses on detoxifying your body, which also includes your brain, it's safe to say that you can have a joyful life with the help of this diet.

Ayurvedic Eating Guidelines

Oh yeah, you can forget about binge-eating while awkwardly sitting on your couch in the middle of the night. Nope, if you want a healthy life, eat healthy too. Nope, I'm not talking about just eating healthy food. But I'm emphasizing developing healthy eating habits too. Oh no, these are not my personal rules but prescribed by Ayurveda itself.

Before discussing these eating guidelines, I want to tell you a bit about how they helped me. See, until a few years ago, I used to be very dull, lethargic, and lacked discipline. It only changed when I followed these guidelines. Now, I'm an energetic person who also possesses strict discipline in life. This has helped me in many aspects of my life. So, yeah, these guidelines are important, so focus!

Eat Naturally

No, I'm not just asking you to eat natural foods while avoiding processed foods. But I'm asking you to eat foods that are grown naturally.

You see, now, most of our food is grown using harmful chemicals and pesticides. Most of the vegetables and fruits are hybrids, which lack proper amounts of nutrients and vitamins. If you eat such food, it doesn't really make any difference. So, try to eat natural food, which has been grown naturally.

Now, there are many supermarkets and stores that sell organic fruits and vegetables. You can visit, and they shop your groceries there, for natural food.

Include Spices

If you think all those spices do is add aroma and flavor, you're wrong, my friend! Spices benefit you much more than you can imagine. They promote digestion, improve your immune system, and most importantly, contain anti-inflammatory elements.

Moreover, spices make any food delicious. So, if you're tired of eating bland food, add a few suitable spices, and make it tasty while keeping it healthy as well.

Drink Water, Appropriately

You can survive even without consuming food for a few days, but lack of proper dehydration can cause serious damage to your body.

Yes, under certain circumstances, water is even more important than food. Ayurveda has a few rules for you when it comes to drinking water.

First and foremost, have a glass of lukewarm water right after you wake up in the morning. This promotes good bowel movements, making it easy for you to evacuate waste.

Then, try to avoid drinking water while you're eating food. Eating and drinking simultaneously can affect your digestive system. So, drink water only after some time as you finish your meal. Also, don't drink water right before you have your food as well.

Other than that, drink water regularly throughout your day to stay hydrated.

Nurture Conscious Eating

Most of us lack discipline, enthusiasm, and energy in our busy lives. This has something to do with the way we eat, as well.

Most of us love to binge-watch Netflix and binge-eat whatever we have around us. That's not so healthy, is it?

Well, try to plan your meals, and try to have them at the same time every day. This cultivates a healthy eating habit, which also keeps you disciplined and grounded.

Also, try to express your gratitude for the food you're eating, whether it's praying to your god or simply the Universe itself. You do you!

Try Experimenting with Your Food

Oh no, Ayurveda is not some fixed and rigid health system. Although it comes with its own set of rules, you don't have to shy away from experimenting with your food.

Actually, Ayurveda promotes experimentation. However, while doing so, keep your dosha in mind. Don't try to include too many ingredients that may cause your doshic imbalance.

Other than that, you don't have to worry much here. Also, experimenting with what you eat adds excitement to your day. Try tweaking the recipes according to your liking, and see how it goes. I regularly do that and came up with some amazing Ayurvedic recipes, which my family and friends crave for.

Cooking Guidelines

Apart from eating guidelines, Ayurveda also suggests several cooking guidelines as well. These guidelines are in place to help you cook healthy, clean, and tasty food.

In the first several years of my Ayurvedic journey, I honestly didn't bother much about these guidelines. However, I started following them after some time and found great benefits from them. So, here are the main Ayurvedic cooking guidelines:

Clean Your Ingredients Thoroughly

Oh yeah, you may be thinking, why bother cleaning them, since they're going to be cooked in heat, right?! Well, here's the thing! Vegetables and fruits have germs on the surface, and the heat kills them off.

I know! But, what about the chemicals that peacefully lay on the surface of your food items? Well, the cooking heat doesn't do much about them, right? This is exactly why you need to clean the ingredients thoroughly before cooking them.

Moreover, what would you lose when you clean them for a couple of minutes, huh?!

Wash Your Crockery Properly

This isn't something you didn't know already, isn't it?! However, do you take it seriously, cleaning your cooking pans, vessels, and other crockery items?

If your cooking vessels still contain remnants of leftover food, which could well be turned into toxins already, you're risking your health. So, try to spend a few more minutes properly cleaning your crockery set before cooking.

Avoiding Deep-Frying Your Food

I know, I know, deep-fried food is extremely tasty. However, when you deep-fry your food, it loses most of the valuable vitamins and nutrients.

Here, you can find a middle ground. Rather than directly frying your food, try boiling it first and then frying it.

By doing so, you can save those key nutrients and vitamins completely from evaporating, as the boiled vegetables or leaves retain most of these elements. For a weekend meal, you can have your own way, since you deserve to eat delicious food, even though it's not really healthy, once in a while.

Ayurvedic Way of Eating

Okay, now, it's time to talk about planning your diet, according to the Ayurveda. This amazing ancient science has already identified thousands of years ago that not every human body is the same, and each is unique in its own way.

Based on that fact, Ayurveda suggests eating according to their body type. This can be done by getting yourself informed about the six tastes of Ayurveda, along with the importance of Dosha-specific eating. And that's exactly what we're going to discuss now.

The Six Tastes

Ayurveda stresses having your food, which consists of the six important tastes or flavors. These tastes not only stimulate your taste buds but also provides you many nutritional benefits as well.

If you eat your food with all these tastes, you can stay very healthy, according to Ayurveda. So, here are those tastes, their benefits, and their qualities.

Sweet

Who doesn't love having sweet-flavored foods? This flavor is made of water and earth elements, making it helpful in sensing similar qualities. It is descending and heavy, and also, at the same time, cold and wet.

Sweet is also the taste of sharing, love, and compassion. As it comes from natural sugars, it is also full of energy. Several fats, proteins, and Carbohydrates are known to possess this flavor. Fruits and herbs with this taste nourish us, as foods such as licorice and beetroot, along with rice, honey, and milk, are highly beneficial to our health.

Sour

This flavor is made of fire and earth elements. This taste is known to be oily, hot, and also light. It enhances your digestive system and helps in clearing your taste buds, along with the sides of your tongue.

You can find this flavor in foods such as citrus fruits, vinegar, sour cream, yoghurt, bread, wine, and several others. Sour foods often make your mouth moist, which also increases the free flow of saliva. This not only helps your digestion but also awaken your emotions too.

Salt

Made of fire and water elements, the Salt taste is considered to create heat and moisture. When used in appropriate quantities, it makes our food very tasty. However, when used in incorrect quantities, it can also spoil the taste of your food. Such a tricky flavor, I'd say!

This flavor helps in calming your nervous system and also promotes overall stability. When you consume an excess of salt, it may negatively impact your emotions, causing desire and greed. So, use it cautiously.

Pungent

This flavor is a blend of air and fire elements, with light and dry qualities. Do you know that there are dedicated receptors on your tongue to perceive this flavor?

Our tongue senses this flavor through the irritation of nerve endings and tissues—the heat of spicy foods spread across your whole body, which makes it a very crucial flavor. Too much of this taste causes negative emotions such as anger and intolerance.

However, this flavor is very good for digestion. It also helps you in dealing with inflammation as well, while promoting good metabolism. Onions, garlic, and chilies are some of the prominent foods that contain this flavor. Oh, how can I forget about the whole family of spices that come with taste?

Bitter

Both air and space elements are in abundance in the bitter flavor. This taste has dry, cool, and light qualities. Most plants are rich in this flavor. The reason for it is that plants need this flavor for their self-defense mechanism.

The receptors on the back of your tongue are responsible for perceiving this flavor. You can find this flavor in leafy vegetables such as kale, spinach, and rocket, spices such as turmeric, dandelion, and fenugreek. Tea, Coffee, along with several fruits such as olives, grapefruits, and bitter melon, also have this flavor.

This flavor helps in getting rid of excess amounts of drying fluids in your body. It also helps in the overall detoxification process. However, too much consumption of this flavor can leave you feeling anxious and fearful.

Astringent

The driest flavor of all, Astringent is made of air and earth elements. It is often dry and heavy. Whenever you eat something with this taste, your mouth contracts, which also brings mucus membranes closer.

This flavor is mostly found in tannins, which are a type of plant compound. Legumes such as lentils and beans, fruits such as pears, cranberries, and pomegranates, and vegetables such as cauliflower, turnip, and broccoli are rich in astringent. This flavor promotes wound healing by removing excess fluid and swelling.

Eating According to Your Dosha

Other than the Taste factor, you should also focus on maintaining the diet suitable to your dosha. Once you identify your dominant dosha, you can simply plan your food according to it.

Ayurveda says that balancing your dosha is highly important for a healthy life. In that, food plays a crucial role. Eating unsuitable food may cause doshic imbalance while consuming suitable food helps you in balancing your dosha.

Vata Diet

All Vata people should avoid eating too much of cold foods like iced drinks, salads, raw greens, and vegetables. You may also consider avoiding excess consumption of candies and coffee.

Vata types must focus on eating foods that have sweet, sour, and salty flavors. Foods such as warm soups, milk, stew, hot cereals, butter, cream, raw nuts, and freshly baked bread are good for Vata people.

Pitta Diet

If you're a Pitta, try avoiding foods such as cream, cheese, and pickles. Also, try consuming fewer amounts of salty, oily, and hot foods.

Instead, try eating foods that are warm or cool with sweet, bitter, and astringent flavors. Foods such as cinnamon toast, cold cereal, apple tea, salads, ice cream, tea, vegetables are good for you.

Kapha Diet

For Kapha-dominated people, foods that are too fatty or sweet is a no-go. They also need to keep an eye on their salt consumption. Don't eat too much of foods like chilled foods, fats, sugars, and dairy products.

However, Kaphas can eat food items that are light, warm, and dry. Try to eat food items such as endive, romaine lettuce, and any food that's prepared using dry cooking methods such as grilling, baking, or broiling.

Ayurvedic Staples

Here are some of the most commonly used and eaten Ayurvedic staples:

Almonds: Rich in protein, provides strength to body and mind.

Ginger: Helps in settling down your stomach, promotes digestion, and detoxifies the body.

Leafy, Green Vegetables: Rich in nutrients and vitamins,

along with calcium, iron, and magnesium.

Seasonal Fruits: Packed with minerals, vitamins, and antioxidants. Helps in better digestion.

Ghee: Aids in better transportation of nutrients throughout the body. Also enhances the digestive system.

Lemon: Contains high amounts of minerals and vitamins—also, a detoxifying agent.

Cumin Seeds: Helps in digestion, also adds delicious flavor to your food.

Dates & Figs: Offers high amounts of energy, rich in minerals such as calcium and magnesium.

Ayurvedic Recipes

Healing Recipes

Thousands of years ago, the great Ayurvedic sage, Charaka, in his books, wrote that our kitchen is our pharmacy and our pantry is all about medicine.

Now, what are healing foods? Any food that's believed to be good for us that promotes overall health, like the doctors, suggest eating foods that are rich in fiber, vitamins, natural sugars like fructose. Simply put, healing foods are light and are healthy. They reduce cholesterol, control our blood sugars, reduce bone loss, thereby saving us from these fatal diseases like cardiovascular issues, diabetes, osteoporosis, combat infections, and lessen inflammation, prevent longstanding diseases that stay with us for life. Well, I'm not here to scare you, but to give you some scrumptious recipes. Let's get started!

Pepo Summer Salad

Cucumbers are not just for tasty pickles and treating dark circles but are great for summer salads, too, as they are extremely cooling and hydrating. This pepo salad is one of my go-to comfort foods during summer, and you can try this salad any time of the year, as cucumbers are available year-round. This salad will keep you as cool as a cucumber.

Ingredients:

5 Persian cucumbers

2 large green beans

1 arugula

Half head chopped romaine lettuce

1 cup of cooked quinoa

Juice of 1 lemon

2 tablespoons of virgin olive oil

1 bunch of fresh dill

1 bunch of fresh cilantro

5 - 10 fresh mint leaves

Salt for seasoning

Pinch of ground black pepper for seasoning

Preparation:

1. Chop the cucumbers, romaine lettuce, green beans and

keep them in a salad bowl.

2. Toss in the arugula, cooked quinoa into a salad bowl.

3. In a small bowl, add the lime juice, olive oil into it and tear the mint, dill, and cilantro. Mix them all into the dressing. Add salt and pepper to it.

4. Top the salad with dressing and toss them and serve.

Miso Asparagus Soup

Japanese people are known for their high life expectancy due to low rates of heart diseases and cancer in the world. If the Japanese believe that this soup has healing power, we should simply try it and include this in our diet with zero questions asked. But you might be wondering how does this recipe fits in the Ayurvedic recipe list. I wanted to add this recipe because this recipe embodies the principles of Ayurveda.

Ingredients:

5 cups of vegetable broth or stock

Grate one medium fresh ginger

1 bunch of chopped asparagus

1 cup of soft tofu

3 tablespoons of white or yellow-colored miso

Tamari, for flavoring

Preparation:

1. In a large saucepan, add broth and bring it to a boil at medium to high heat.

2. Add in the ginger and cover the pan and turn it to low heat and boil for 10 minutes.

3. It's time for the asparagus and tofu to go into the broth, then simmer it and cook until the asparagus is tender, for about 3-5 minutes.

4. Now shut down the heat and ladle one-fourth of the

broth into a large bowl and add in the miso. Whisk it and mix this into the soup.

5. Add tamari to enhance the flavor. Serve hot!

Curried Beans

Curry leaves are a staple seasoning in the Indian kitchen for ages. I have been growing curry plants and eating curry leaves for my entire life now. Curry leaves are highly aromatic and add a lot of flavor to the dish. Indians have been reaping its benefits for a long time now. Let us try to incorporate curry leaf powder as spice blends in our dishes.

Ingredients:

1 pound of chopped green beans

2 tablespoons of ghee

½ teaspoon of mustard seeds

2 teaspoons of salt

1 ginger, finely chopped

½ teaspoon dried curry leaf powder

½ cup coarsely chopped hazelnuts

1 teaspoon tamari

Some freshly black pepper powder, for flavoring

1 bunch chopped Italian parsley

Preparation:

1. In a pot, add water and 1 teaspoon of salt bring it to boil.

2. To the boiling water, add green beans and cook for 2 minutes. Now, in a bowl, fill ice and water. Take out the beans and immerse them in ice and water and cool them.

3. Once cooled, drain them and dry them by placing them on a towel. Take a saucepan and melt 1 tablespoon of

ghee over medium heat.

4. Add mustard seeds, and once they start to pop, add in the ginger and curry leaf powder. Close it with a lid and cook for a minute.

5. Now add the green beans and mix them thoroughly. Place the lid and cook for about 5 minutes.

6. Once the beans are soft, turn off the heat. Add tamari, salt, and pepper as seasonings and mix them.

7. Take a small pan, on medium heat, melt 1 tablespoon of ghee. To this, add the hazelnuts and stir them till they turn golden.

8. Turn off the heat. Now, top the beans with parsley and hazelnuts. Enjoy!

Roots & Shoots Broth

In the concept of macrobiotics, Japanese cuisine has a healing broth made of a root, round, and a shoot. The root has veggies like lotus root, carrots, daikon radish, sweet potato, ginger, and round stands for veggies like onion, beet, garlic. Lastly, the veggies that grow above the land are considered shoots like bamboo shoots, chard, celery, kale, bok choy, or Spinach. According to this Japanese concept, you get the benefits and energies from above, below, and around you that aid in healing.

Ingredients:

1 beetroot

1 celery stalk

1 daikon radish

4 cups of water

1 ginger

Pinch salt

Fresh black pepper powder

Preparation:

1. Roughly chop the radish, beetroot, and celery, and finely chop the ginger.

2. Add these veggies along with water, salt, and pepper to a soup pot.

3. Bring it to a boil and then turn down the heat to low and simmer for 15 minutes.

4. Strain and serve the broth; you can also keep it in a thermos to sip all day.

Cauliflower Chickpea Patties

Cauliflower is one of the most underrated vegetables; you will be surprised by the impressive nutritional profile it has. But most importantly, the fiber in it will make you want to try this recipe.

Did you know a medium head of it has 12 grams of fiber! And chickpeas also have about 9 - 12 grams of fiber per every 100 grams of them. Those facts make this our go-to fiber-rich recipe.

Ingredients:

1 cauliflower head (florets)

1 cup of rinsed chickpeas

1 diced bell pepper

1 diced onion

2 minced garlic cloves

1 tsp turmeric

1 cup Panko bread crumbs

1 tsp cumin

Salt, pepper to taste

Preparation:

1. Preheat the oven to 375 and steam or boil the florets until soft.

2. On low heat, stir fry the onion, bell pepper until soft. To this, add garlic and fry for a minute.

3. Now take a large bowl and smash the chickpeas and florets one after another. Add the rest of all the ingredients and mix well till combined.

4. The mix should be moist to make balls. Now, start making balls carefully. I prefer to have them slightly larger than the golf ball.

5. Press the ball to make a patty. Place these patties on a baking dish or oiled pan. Bake them until brown and flip them in between; it would take about 15- 20 minutes for each side.

Mung Bean Green Soup

Green grams are ayurvedic beauties that are light, sweet, and astringent. These are widely used in India and are ayurvedic kitchen staples. Green grams are the richest source of folic acid. This soup is balanced by cooking with ghee and broth, making it indeed healing.

Ingredients:

1 cup of whole green grams

1 tablespoon of ghee

1 piece of fresh peeled ginger, minced (1 inch)

1 teaspoon fresh black pepper powder

6 cups vegetable broth

1 cup of finely chopped leafy greens

Preparation:

1. Soak green grams for 8 hours. Rinse and drain them.

2. Take a large soup pot and heat on medium heat, and melt the ghee. Add the ginger and black pepper powder

and stir for a minute.

3. Add green grams and broth to this and cover the lid. Bring it to boil on low heat, then turn it to medium and cook for 30 minutes.

4. Lastly, add in the greens and cook for another 10 minutes, or until the beans turn soft.

Asparagus Sesame Stir Fry

Being an Indian, I have grown up seeing older people with joint pains eat sesame seeds. According to modern science, copper is known to reduce pain and inflammation in people suffering from rheumatoid arthritis. To my surprise, sesame seeds are rich in copper. With just 2 tablespoons, we can meet 83 % of our daily required value. Add asparagus, as it's one of the most balanced nutritious vegetables; you should give this recipe a try.

Ingredients:

4 cups chopped asparagus

2 teaspoon chopped ginger

3 teaspoon chopped garlic

2 teaspoon soy sauce

3 teaspoon sesame seeds

1 teaspoon corn flour mixed with half cup water

Pinch of sugar

2 tablespoon oil

Salt to taste

Preparation:

1. Take a frying pan and heat the oil and add ginger, garlic and in a high heat setting, stir fry for 30 seconds.

2. Now add soy sauce and asparagus and toss them well.

3. Add sesame seeds, salt, sugar, and corn flour paste and cook until corn flour coats asparagus for about 2-3 minutes. And serve hot.

Kapha Pacifying Recipes

Kapha dominant people should focus on consuming bitter, pungent, and astringent flavors. Foods that are dry, light, and stimulating to counter the heaviness.

Kaphas need to favor foods that are spicy and are cooked to balance the cold and dry foods like popcorn, toast for the water element. Fruits that are light and citrus, vegetables like leafy greens, legumes, and grains like quinoa, seeds are suitable for Kaphas. Cook them with strong spices like turmeric, ginger, mustard, cinnamon, clove, basil, cayenne, oregano, pepper. Skipping dinner once a week can revive digestion. Consuming a drink made of hot water along with spices like ginger, black pepper, turmeric, and lemon will boost metabolism.

Sprout Green Salad

This sprout green salad has the Ayurvedic staple green gram sprouts and fresh green leafy veggies that are pungent and bitter, which are ideal for balancing Kapha. Sprouts are nutritional powerhouses that contain many active enzymes. This simple salad is light but comforting and meets our daily nutritional values.

Ingredients:

1/4 cup sprouted green gram

2 grated carrots

One bunch of chopped lettuce

Lime juice of 1 lemon

3 tablespoon of olive oil

Salt to taste

Fresh black pepper powder

Preparation:

1. Mix sprouts with the rest of the vegetables.

2. Drizzle the lemon juice or olive oil over it. Add salt for better taste.

3. Toss them well, and it's ready to serve.

Turkish-Thai Soup

Let us take the goodness of this staple from Thai cooking - the most fragrant lemongrass and add a Turkish touch to it with this red lentil soup that is satiating. This soup is soul-warming to Kaphas.

Ingredients:

Lemongrass paste (makes 2/3rd cup):

2 tablespoons of sunflower oil

Half of an onion

2 stalks of lemongrass

1-inch peeled ginger root

1 inch peeled turmeric root or 2 teaspoons of turmeric powder

1 Thai red chili

2 garlic cloves

1 kaffir lime leaf or half teaspoon lemon zest

Soup ingredients:

2 tablespoons of ghee

4 tablespoons of lemongrass paste

Salt to taste

1 teaspoon long pepper powder

2 peeled and chopped tomatoes

130 grams of red lentils

2 tablespoons of lime juice

1 bunch of cilantro

4 cups of water

Preparation:

1. Make the lemongrass paste. Add the onion, sunflower

oil, lemongrass, turmeric, ginger, chili, garlic, kaffir leaf, and garlic into a blender to make a thick paste.

2. To make the soup, take a medium pan and heat on medium heat and warm the ghee.

3. Now, add in the lemongrass paste, long black pepper powder, and salt. Sauté for 30 seconds.

4. Add in the tomato and lentils, lastly add water. Boil over low heat for 10 minutes until lentils are soft and mushy.

5. Lastly, add in the cilantro and lime juice. You can blend it to make puree for a creamy consistency and serve hot.

Pearl Millets Bread (Bajra Roti)

Pearl millets are the most underrated gluten-free grain until today. But ancient Indians consumed Bajra on a daily basis. Bajra has all the potential antioxidants like phenol, phytic acid, tannins, which fight free radicles and help us fight metabolic disorders, prevent aging, cancer, and heart-related issues.

Ingredients:

2oo grams cups of Bajra flour

Ghee to add flavor

Preparation:

1. In a bowl, mix Bajra flour with little water and knead to make a soft dough. Make large balls by dividing the dough into equal parts.

2. Sprinkle some Bajra flour on the dough ball, and roll it out to make rotis (tortillas) with a rolling pin.

3. Place the roti on a hot pan. Keep patting it with water.

4. Flip roti once it dries up and evenly cooked on both sides.

5. Apply ghee on top of it and serve hot.

Chickpea Leafy Greens Curry

If you are someone looking to opt for plant-based protein diets, get your hands on this recipe that has an abundance of plant proteins in it.

Ingredients:

4 cups of roughly chopped baby spinach

1 cup of cooked chickpeas

2 teaspoons of coriander seeds

1 teaspoon cumin seeds

1/2 inch peeled and chopped ginger

2 tablespoons of finely chopped coriander leaves

2 tablespoons of powdered cashew nut

2 tablespoons of mustard oil

Salt to taste

1 tablespoon of lemon juice

Preparation:

1. Roughly chop the spinach and add ginger and coriander leaves to it and cook for five minutes and stir frequently and then turn off.

2. Take a saucepan and warm the ghee. Now, add the coriander, cumin seeds, and stir-fry for 2 minutes.

3. Add the spices to the spinach mix. Mash the mixture by adding water in a masher for a thick paste.

4. Now add the chickpeas and bring the mixture to a boil.

5. Lastly, add the crunchy powdered cashew nuts and turn down the heat. Add some salt and lemon juice for taste.

6. Serve it with pear millet roti or chapatis/tortillas.

Sesame Ginger Laddoo

Sesame seeds are unsung heroes with an abundance of good fats. There's an Assyrian myth that says the night before they created the earth, gods drank sesame wine. Myths aside, from dealing with chronic diseases to new-age problems like stress, this recipe works for all.

Ingredients:

1 cup of freshly roasted black sesame seeds

1 teaspoon ginger powder

1 cup jaggery powder

1 cup of water

1/4 cup cashew nuts powders

1 teaspoon cardamom powder

Preparation:

1. Mash the sesame seeds in pestle and mortar.

2. To this, add ginger and jaggery powders to it.

3. Now, add cashew nuts powders and mix them well.

4. Use some ghee to make round balls or laddoos. Serve them to your loved ones.

Vata Pacifying Diet

Vata is dry, light, and cool. Vata dominant ones should consume foods that are warming, heavy, and oily. These traits are ideal to counter the characteristics of Vatas and promote digestion.

Flavors like salty, sweet, and sour and fruits that are heavy and sweet are ideal and consumed cooked rather than raw. Warming spices like cloves, cumin, sage, ginger, fennel, cardamom, and cinnamon will strengthen and keeps you grounded. High-quality fats are essential for Vata.

Consuming gentle spices like cinnamon, ginger, nutmeg is good to promote digestion. To keep Vatas hydrated and warm, sipping ginger tea all day can help. Eat your three meals at the same time every day; being consistent will improve digestion.

Mixed Root Salad

Ever heard of anthocyanin? It's a potent antioxidant that helps prevent cardiovascular disease, one of the leading causes of sudden death. This mixed root salad has sweet potatoes and carrots, which are rich in anthocyanin. I don't think we need any better reason to try this recipe.

Ingredients:

2 boiled or steamed sweet potatoes

2 blanched carrots

Some mustard microgreens

1 cup freshly grated coconut

Salt to taste

Ghee or olive oil

Preparation:

1. Mix the veggies and add grated coconut and salt to it.

2. Drizzle the ghee or olive oil into the mixture.

3. And lastly, top it with mustard microgreens. Toss it and serve.

Butternut Squash Soup

In this digital world, where everyone from kids to adults is addicted to gadgets, we often forget to take care of our eyes. The amount of eyestrain we face due to blue light is unimaginable. But this squash has carotenoids that help in producing retinoic and retinal acid that promote eye health. Let us try this recipe for healthy eyes.

Ingredients:

1 peeled, seeded, and chopped (1 inch) butternut squash

1 cup peeled, seeded, and chopped red pumpkin

1-inch finely chopped fresh ginger.

1 teaspoon cumin

½ teaspoon turmeric

1 teaspoon cinnamon powder

¼ teaspoon clove

3 cups of water

1 cup of coconut milk

Salt for taste

Pinch of pepper for taste

2 tablespoon ghee

Pinch of nutmeg for garnish

Preparation:

1. Steam or boil the pumpkin and squash.

2. Add in the coconut milk or water and mix, then keep it aside.

3. In a pan, warm the ghee. To this, add the turmeric powder, cumin, ginger, clove, and cinnamon.

4. Now, add these spices to the mixture and mash it. Finally, garnish with nutmeg. Serve hot.

Corn Flat Bread (Makki Ki Roti)

Corn flatbread can be a great choice for gluten intolerants. Although corn is high in good carbs, it is also rich in fiber and gluten-free whole grains. Vatas are thin and light framed, and consuming corn can help them build body. Go team carbs and corns for the gains!

Ingredients:

200 grams of corn flour

Ghee

Salt to taste

Warm water

Preparation:

1. Add warm water and a pinch of salt and knead the corn flour. Make small balls of the dough.

2. Pat them with water and press the dough between palms to make flatbread. You can use butter paper to do these rotis. Make them thicker than usual roti.

3. In a hot pan, cook them on low heat and flip the roti until roasted.

4. Apply some ghee on both sides and serve it with sarson ka saag, which you will learn in the next recipe.

Sarson Ka Saag (Spicy Mustard Leaf Curry)

We all have tried the famous mustard microgreens. For a change, let us eat their shoots and leaves. Mustard greens have compounds that bind bile acids in our digestive system. Bile acids are the ones that absorb fats.

Now blocking the reabsorption of bile acids can lower our cholesterol levels. When mustard greens are steamed, the bile acid-binding effect significantly increases, and cholesterol levels decrease. That's how we are cooking this recipe for a healthy heart.

Ingredients:

2 lbs. finely chopped mustard leaves

1/4 lbs. finely chopped spinach

1 inch of minced ginger

Salt to taste

2 finely chopped green chilies

2 broken red chilies

2 tablespoons ghee

2 tablespoon corn flour

Preparation:

1. Steam both the greens until soft, and add green chilies and salt to it.

2. Add water and mash the leaves, and set aside.

3. On a pan, warm the ghee. To this, add green chilies, red chilies, and ginger and sauté for 2 minutes.

4. Add this to the mashed leaves and stir the mixture.

5. Now make corn flour slurry by mixing corn flour and water, and add it to the mixture, and simmer for 30 minutes.

6. Serve with cornbread from the previous recipe (Makki ki roti).

Carrot Pudding (Carrot Halwa)

The famous Punjabi Gajar ka halwa is a luscious pudding that can be a great dessert of choice for gatherings. The carotenoid-rich carrots give us healthy eyes and protect from cataract. Combine this with vanilla ice-cream for enhanced taste during parties.

Ingredients:

5 grated carrots

1/4 teaspoon cardamom powder

3 tablespoons of ghee

10- 15 cashews

4 cups of milk

1/4 cup jaggery

10 raisins

Pinch of saffron

Preparation:

1. Add 2 tablespoon ghee and cook carrots on medium heat for 20 minutes or until carrots are soft.

2. To this, add milk and mix it well and boil the mixture until milk is completely absorbed by the carrots.

3. Add the jaggery powder and saffron. Let it cook for 15 minutes.

4. Meanwhile, in a small pan, add 1 tablespoon ghee and roast the cashews and raisins for 2 minutes and add cardamom powder to it and mix this with carrots and serve hot.

Pitta Balancing Recipes

Pitta dominant people should consume foods that taste sweet, astringent, and bitter with foods that soothe, cool, and sustain. Foods that are cool and dry to balance the fiery and watery nature of pittas. Consume high-quality fat like ghee—cooling herbs like cilantro, mint, dill, and fennel. Use sweet and bitter fruits and vegetables like beets, and bitter melons, sweet and white potatoes. Hydrate yourself with cucumber, lime, and mint water and sip through your day.

Sweet Bitter Salad

Quinoa seeds are a package of all good things. Quinoa is one of the fewer plant sources that are a complete protein. It has a whopping 8 grams of protein in one cup of cooked quinoa. It has all nine amino acids that play a crucial role in most systems in our body.

Ingredients:

1 cup quinoa

1 large lemon

2 cups of water

1/4 teaspoon coriander powder

1/4 teaspoon cumin powder

1/4 teaspoon sweet paprika

2 ripe avocados chopped into 1 inch

Fresh black pepper powder

Salt to taste

Preparation:

1. Rinse and cook the quinoa with water. Once it's fluffy, strain it and set it aside.

2. Once cooled, add the avocado chunks to it and add lemon juice to it.

3. Lastly, add salt and all the spices. Toss and serve.

Pumpkin, Herbs & Spices Soup

Alongside making our Halloween decorations, pumpkins also keep our bodies healthy. Albino pumpkin is rich in zinc and carotenoids, which protect men from prostate enlargement. Pumpkins, being rich in antioxidants, prevent peptic ulcers and asthma attacks. Pumpkin is rich in L-tryptophan, amino acid, and its deficiency is associated with depression. This pumpkin and green gram combo soothes and calms our mind and body. Let's try this out.

Ingredients:

1 cup finely sliced albino pumpkin

1 cup chopped (1 inch) green beans

1/4 cup green gram

1/4-inch fresh grated ginger

1/4 teaspoon of cumin powder

Pinch of turmeric

1/4 teaspoon of fresh black pepper powder

1/4 teaspoon of coriander powder

Finely chopped fresh herbs like parsley, rosemary, mint, or thyme to taste

Preparation:

1. Steam the pumpkin and beans for 20 minutes.

2. Cook green grams separately until soft and mushy, then add this to the veggies.

3. Add in the spices and herbs.

4. Mash the mixture and serve hot.

Green Beans Ginger Curry

We rarely have green beans in our minds when it comes to planning a meal, and if you are one among them, then you are missing on the major benefits this veggie has to offer. This recipe offers you 12 grams of fiber for 3 cups of beans. It is rich in folate. Beans are rich in potassium, which helps ease tension in our blood vessels and lower blood pressure.

<u>Ingredients:</u>

3 cups of chopped green beans

2 tablespoons fresh minced ginger

1/2 cup of water

2 tablespoons of ghee

Pinch of hing

1 teaspoon turmeric

1/2 teaspoon mustard seeds

Salt to taste

Lemon juice

Preparation:

1. In a pan, add water, salt and boil the beans until tender. Warm the ghee and add the spices.

2. Let the mustard seeds pop and add ginger; sauté for a minute and transfer this to the beans and mix them well and sprinkle the lemon juice, and it's ready to serve.

Milk and Rice Kheer

This rice pudding is a customary Indian recipe for festivals and served as Prasadham (offerings) at Hindu temples. This nourishing recipe is a pacifier for high digestive fire and bleeding disorders. Red rice shines in its rich antioxidants and decreases inflammation in the body.

Ingredients:

1/2 cup red rice

1 teaspoon cashew nuts

1 teaspoon raisins

4 cups of milk

1 teaspoon rose water

1 teaspoon ghee

3 green cardamoms

1/2 cup jaggery

Preparation:

1. Soak the rice for 2 hours in water. Drain it and add rice into the milk and let it boil.

2. Once the mixture thickens, add the jaggery.

3. In a pan, warm ghee and sauté the cashews until they turn golden brown.

4. Then, sauté the raisins and let them swell and add them to the mixture, add rose water and mix. Serve hot.

Almond Dates Shake

This frothy shake has powerful ingredients that nurture our whole body. The cinnamon and date combo is potential demulcent expectorants that help our throat by soothing and clear our respiratory tract by eliminating thick mucus. Although dates are heavy on our tummy, the ginger in this shake makes it easy to digest.

Ingredients:

1 cup almonds

100 ml of cow milk/ coconut milk

1 tablespoon ghee

2 dried dates soaked overnight

Pinch of cinnamon

1 inch of fresh ginger

Preparation:

1. Blend the almonds and water to make homemade almond milk.

2. Remove the pits in dates.

3. Warm the cow milk and add dates and blend them all.

4. And lastly, add ghee and serve.

Immunity Boosting Recipes

In these uncertain times, we realize the importance of good immunity. These recipes are aimed to help prevent common and untreatable problems where cure lies in prevention, and the path to prevention lies in boosting our immunity.

Ginger Broccolini

As the burden of cancer on humans is increasing day by day, all we can do is boost our immunity. There's a saying that claims "cancer hates cabbage," which is a fact, and cancer hates the entire list of cruciferous veggies, like broccoli, cauliflower, arugula, kale, Brussels sprouts, bok choy, collards, watercress, and mustard greens. This entire family of veggies produces anti-cancer chemicals. Let's try this recipe out for this anti-cancer goodness.

Ingredients:

1 bunch of broccolini

1 tablespoon of minced ginger

1 tablespoon of ghee

1 tablespoon of lemon juice

1 teaspoon of lemon zest

Ground black pepper

Salt for seasoning

Preparation:

1. In a large pot, add salt, water, and broccolini and cook for 2 minutes. Fill another bowl with ice and water.

2. After 2 minutes, drain the broccolini and put it in the ice water.

3. Now, in a skillet, melt the ghee over medium heat and add in the zest and ginger.

4. Drain the broccolini and add it to this and cook for 2 minutes and turn off the heat.

5. Lastly, add the salt and pepper, drizzle some lemon juice and toss.

Basil Pesto

Let us give this traditional Italian dish an Ayurvedic spin. Pesto is power-packed with phytochemicals of basil, and healthy fats from pine nuts aids in a healthy heart, brain and keeps our blood sugars normal. Serve it with toast by adding it into the avocado mash or as a spread to your favorite dish.

Ingredients:

1 cup fresh basil leaves

1 tablespoon pine nuts

Pinch of asafetida

1 garlic clove

1 teaspoon turmeric

2 tablespoons extra-virgin olive oil

Preparation:

The authentic taste of the pesto lies in crushing it; I can't stress enough the usage of marble motor pestle. It is typically made from crushing it, and it gives a more intense flavor than the pesto made in food processors. But if you want to go easy and use a food processor, use the "timing the pour" technique. Pulse the basil, garlic, pine nuts into a puree. Put the puree in a serving bowl and stir; drizzle the olive oil.

Ginger, Lemon & Honey Tea

This medicinal tea has pungent, sweet, and sour flavors in it. I have been taking it with me on the days I travel so that I boost my immune system and fall sick less often when I'm not in the comfort of my home. Sipping through this tea during flu season will keep you healthy.

Ingredients:

1-inch fresh grated ginger

4 cups of water

1 lemon

2 tablespoons of raw honey

Preparation:

Bring the water to boil and add ginger on low heat and

simmer for 5 minutes. Turn down the heat and let it cool for 2 minutes and squeeze the lemon juice into it. Strain the tea to remove ginger. Add the honey and enjoy the warm tea.

Cinnamon–Honey Syrup

This recipe is a boon for people with bronchitis and works wonders for sore throat, cough, and heavy mucus. Consume this syrup every hour like we do tonics.

When suffering from a cough, add this syrup and 1 tablespoon lemon juice into warm water and sip this tea throughout the day. Consuming one spoonful of this syrup before meals strengthens digestion.

Ingredients:

4 tablespoons of raw honey

½ teaspoon cloves powder

1 minced ginger

½ teaspoon cinnamon powder

1 tablespoon lemon juice

Preparation:

1. Soften the honey by placing a small bowl of honey in a larger hot water bowl.

2. Once the honey is soft, add cinnamon, ginger, cloves, lemon juice, and mix well.

3. Keep it aside for 30 minutes; lemon works as a thinning agent for honey.

4. Store this at room temperature in an airtight container.

Mango-Coconut Crumble

Summer calls for the king of fruits – Mango. Let us include this recipe for mango maniacs. Make sure to use ripe mangoes for a sweet, juicy, and tangy flavor. You can enjoy this mango treat for breakfast as it contains only a tablespoon of sugar per serving.

Ingredients:

50 ml of fresh, homemade coconut milk

4 chopped mangoes

2 tablespoons of fresh lime juice

2 teaspoons of vanilla extract

3 tablespoons of maple syrup

1/2 cup coconut sugar

Pinch of Salt

1/2 cup of shredded coconut

1 teaspoon cardamom powder

1/4 cup coconut oil

Preparation:

1. In a bowl, combine 1 tablespoon lime juice with coconut milk and keep it aside to sour.

2. Now, warm up the oven to 350 F. In a large bowl, add maple syrup of 1 tablespoon and mangoes, vanilla extract, salt, lime juice. Pour this filling into an 8- by-8-inch pie dish and spread evenly.

3. Take a medium bowl, add coconut sugar, shredded coconut, a pinch of salt, cardamom. Oil your hands with coconut oil and work until the mixture is moist enough.

4. Add soured coconut milk and 2 tablespoons of maple syrup.

5. Crumble this mixture over the mango filling and bake for 30 minutes. Serve for breakfast along with bananas or berries.

Amla Juice

The 2500 old miracle formula Ayurvedic sages left us is the recipe of chayvanprash. Amla is a primary ingredient and base of this powerful immunity booster. It is rich in vitamin C, making it a must-have, daily juice.

Ingredients:

3-4 chopped Indian gooseberry

200 ml of water

Pinch of salt

Pinch of pepper

2 - 3 tablespoons Manuka honey

Preparation:

Blend the amla in water and strain the pulp and discard it. Now add pepper, salt, and Makuna honey and mix well. You can add this juice to buttermilk and consume it during afternoons.

Pregnancy Recipes

Giving birth can be joyful and overwhelming at the same time. Making dietary changes and dealing with morning sickness can take a toll on us. It is important to set a goal to eat nutritious foods, remember you are eating for two, so maximizing prenatal nutrition is a must.

Ideally, pregnant women's plates should have one-fourth of it with whole grains, one-fourth of it with dairy products and lean protein, and half of the plates with vegetables and fruits. Consuming fruits and veggies is extremely important during second and third trimesters. The rule of thumb of eating during pregnancy is including sources that have folic acid, calcium, iron, and protein in each meal. Most of the carb choices for each day should be made from whole grains. These recipes I curated for you are a nutritious choice during pregnancy.

Spinach Paneer

Spinach is loaded with folate, and paneer is bursting with calcium, which makes this creamy combo a must-try during pregnancy to avoid brain, spine, and bone defects.

Ingredients:

2 cups of cubed paneer or soft tofu

1 tablespoon ghee

4 cups of chopped and steamed spinach

1/2 cup coconut milk

1 teaspoon coriander powder

1 teaspoon black pepper powder

1/4 teaspoon ground nutmeg

Preparation:

1. Pulse the steamed spinach into the puree and set aside.

2. In a large saucepan, melt the ghee over medium heat and add in the coriander and black pepper powder, and nutmeg, and sauté them for a minute.

3. Add the spinach puree and coconut milk.

4. Turn down the heat to low and cook uncovered for 5 minutes.

5. Add paneer or soft tofu into the spinach mixture and cook for another 2 minutes.

6. Turn off the heat and add lemon juice. Serve with bread.

Kale, Bottle Gourd, and Apple Juice

Kale is one of the nutrient-dense leaves rich in vitamin C and the richest source of vitamin K in the world. This recipe, including kale, bottle gourds, and apples, is a great immunity booster that promotes a healthy heart, normalizes blood sugar, and aids in weight loss. It's a great choice to drink it during both the prenatal and postnatal periods.

Ingredients:

2 cups of chopped spinach

1 cup of torn kale

1 cup chopped green apple

1 cup chopped bottle gourd

1/4 cup chopped Indian gooseberry

1 tablespoon honey

2 cups of water

Preparation:

Combine all the ingredients in a blender along with 2 cups of water and blend to make juice. Serve at room temperature.

Mashed Roasted Roots

The humble Parsnips are often underrated but are super healthy foods. Being rich in potassium can prevent pregnancy-related hypertension. And the 4.9 grams of fiber for 100 grams takes care of alleviating blood sugars and horrible constipation during pregnancy.

Ingredients:

2 among these root vegetables, like carrots, turnips, sweet potatoes, rutabagas, parsnips

1/2 cup coconut milk

1 tablespoon of ghee

1/2 teaspoon ground ginger

1/2 teaspoons ground cardamom

1/2 teaspoon ground fenugreek

1 teaspoon freshly grated nutmeg

1/2 teaspoon ground cinnamon

Pinch of Salt

Pinch of black pepper powder

Preparation:

1. Warm up the oven to 475 F.

2. With a fork, prick the vegetables several times and place them on a baking sheet. Roast for 45 minutes or until soft.

3. Remove them and let them cool for five minutes.

4. Peel them and put them into a blender and add coconut milk, spices, ghee, and pulse them to achieve a creamy consistency. Add salt and pepper.

Stuffed Dates

Consuming dates in the last few weeks of pregnancy can reduce labor time. Dates have an exceptional ability to promote cervical dilation and natural labor. The compounds in dates mimic the effects of oxytocin, which is responsible for labor contractions and tannins to facilitate contractions, and sugars in dates give you energy during delivery.

Ingredients:

8-10 Medjool dates

1 cup of ghee

1 tablespoon cinnamon powder

1 tablespoon nutmeg powder

1 tablespoon cardamom powder

4 teaspoons of almond butter

Pinch of salt

Lime zest and orange zest for garnish

Preparation:

1. Slice the dates to remove the pits so that we can stuff

the filling.

2. Now open the dates and spoon in almond butter. Line them on a serving plate.

3. In a bowl, mix the spice powders and sprinkle them on the dates. Garnish with the zest and salt.

4. Now add some warm ghee on top of them and enjoy them. You can store these stuffed dates in a jar full of ghee.

Yam Fries

Yam is a storehouse of folate, and yam is rich in vitamin B6 and is known for cure morning sickness, reduce emesis, and preventing low birth weights. It is rich in calcium, iron, zinc, copper, which, in turn, prevents premature births.

Ingredients:

1 yam

2 teaspoons cornstarch

1 tablespoon coconut oil

1 tablespoon ground ginger

1 tablespoon black pepper

1 tablespoon cinnamon powder

1 tablespoon salt

1 tablespoon ground ginger

1 tablespoon turmeric powder

Preparation:

1. Scrub the yam, chop it into ¼-inch-thick for fries. Soak them in a bowl of cold water for 1 hour.

2. Preheat the oven to 425F. In a skillet, warm the coconut oil over medium heat, add in all the spices and

stir for a minute.

3. Take the yam fries into a bowl along with cornstarch and toss.

4. Pour the spicy coconut oil over and give fries a good shake. Arrange the fries in a single layer on the baking sheet, bake for about 15 minutes, and flip.

5. Now, bake for 10-15 minutes or until they turn brown. Turn off the oven and carefully remove and add salt and toss the fries.

6. Let the fries release steam and cool for 10 minutes. Serve them warm.

Fenugreek Paratha

In India, lactating mothers are always advised to consume water-soaked fenugreek seeds to boost breast milk. Which is scientifically proven to improve lactation. In mothers, it prevents gestational diabetes. It's rich in folate and vitamin B12, which help brain development and avoid neural defects in the baby. This recipe is nutritious and makes a good dinner meal.

Ingredients:

2 cups of wheat flour

1 cup finely chopped fenugreek leaves

1/4 cup of sour yoghurt

Half teaspoon turmeric

Half teaspoon red chili powder

1/4 teaspoon cumin powder

1 teaspoon ginger paste

1/2 teaspoon carom seeds

Salt to taste

2 teaspoons coconut oil

5 teaspoons of ghee

Water to knead the dough

Preparation:

1. In a large bowl, add in the wheat flour and fenugreek leaves, curd, all spices, and salt to taste, coconut oil, and mix them well. Curd removes the bitterness of fenugreek leaves.

2. Now add some water start kneading the dough. Cover the dough with a moist cloth and let it rest for 30 minutes.

3. Now make parathas with a rolling pin. Heat the pan and place the paratha and cook for one minute on each side. Now brush a good amount of ghee on both sides and serve it with any curry, pickles, or raitha.

Asparagus Egg Tortillas

This combo is a superfood that's rich in proteins and fewer calories. Eggs are rich in choline, which helps brain cell function and development of brain health, and asparagus is rich in folate. This recipe makes a great choice for breakfast.

Ingredients:

2 egg whites

1 egg

1 tablespoon cheese

4 sliced asparagus spears

1 teaspoon pepper

1 tablespoon milk

Pinch of salt

1 chopped onion

2 teaspoon butter

1 whole wheat tortilla

Preparation:

1. In a bowl, add in the eggs, milk, cheese, and pepper and whisk them.

2. Take a pan and medium over medium heat and add 1 tablespoon butter, asparagus.

3. Now add a pinch of salt, cook, and stir for 5 minutes. Take them onto a plate.

4. Now, in the same skillet, melt the butter on medium heat. Pour in the egg mixture and keep pushing the cooked portion towards the center to cook evenly.

5.Once the omelet is thick enough, add the asparagus and green onions on one side of the omelet and fold in half. Serve in a warm tortilla.

Foods During Infancy

To all the overwhelmed moms, I understand that this responsibility is hard and joyful at the same time. From being sleep deprived of changing diapers a zillion times, time just flies by. So, by the end of 6 months, mothers should figure out all nutritious foods to be fed from thereafter. Ayurveda advises breastfeeding for 6 months and up to 2 years. Around six months old, the baby's teeth begin to erupt, and that's a sign that the baby is ready to eat soft food.

The baby should be introduced to one food at a time. Baby can be fed root vegetables, grains, and legumes until around 12 months of age. Green grams and adzuki beans are easily digestible and most nutritious of all. Start with roots like carrots, beets, and celery. Avoid tomatoes and eggplant.

At all costs, avoid the fancy baby foods from grocery stores. Avoid foods that have multiple food items in them that claim to be nutritious. The worst thing we can do is feed our baby with different foods in a single meal. The digestive fire of a baby needs to figure out and digest them. According to Ayurveda, the fruit doesn't give strength. And should be fed only as a supplement and not as main food till 12 months. Give them fruits when the baby is constipated or excreting hard stools.

When do you think is the right time for you to stop breastfeeding? When the baby is around 18 months, start limiting the number of feedings. By this time, they would most likely understand your words and actions, so let babies off your breast while sleeping and start with bedtime stories. This is when the father should chip in with lots of cuddles and snuggles.

A woman's breasts can produce an adequate amount of milk to feed her baby. Here are some superfoods that improve the thickness of milk. They are fenugreek seeds, garlic, sesame seeds, and red lentils.

With their tiny little hands, babies try to reach our plate. But remember, they can't digest all foods that we can, even if it's mashed. Now please don't introduce baby foods from the grocery store no matter how good the rating is. They have lots of preservatives and synthetic sugars. Babes might enjoy them, but there's nothing better than a rich platter of homemade food for babies. Introduce light foods and well mashed to avoid choking.

At 7 months of age, introduce vegetable soups like carrots, beetroot, pumpkin, bottle gourd, ridge gourd, spinach drumsticks. Make a puree or clear soup. Remember to strain the fiber. Avoid vegetables like cauliflower and cabbage. They might upset their tummy. Fruits are a great choice as supplements. Mash fruits like papaya, banana, mango and feed them fresh. Boil the slices of apple and make them into a puree. Keep an eye on their poop to decide which food is suiting them.

Kitchari for Babies

At 8 months of age, a baby can be fed with full meals like kitchari, rice, mung beans, and vegetables like carrots, peas, beets, pumpkin, spinach, potatoes, beans. Here is a recipe for kitchari for your baby. Here, I am using white rice since it is easily digestible than brown rice and adding spices like ajwain to make digestion easy. Add one different vegetable each day to make this recipe non-boring for the baby.

Ingredients:

1 small cup of white rice

Half cup mung beans

1 cup of water

Chop or grate any of the above-mentioned vegetables

2 tablespoon ghee

5 curry leaves

Half teaspoon of carob powder

Half teaspoon of pepper powder

Pinch of pepper powder

Pinch of salt

Half teaspoon cumin powder

Preparation:

1. Wash the mung beans and rice twice and let them soak for 1 hour. Chop vegetables freshly and add them to the cooker along with rice, mung beans, and water, and salt; cook until soft.

2. Once ready, turn it off and add the spices (optional) and ghee while it's hot and mash them. If needed, add warm water to achieve soft consistency and mash or make a puree.

At 9 months of age, babies are ready to be fed with a hard-boiled egg. And when the baby turns, one baby can be fed with cow milk, remember than cow milk is hard to digest for the baby before they turn one.

At one, introduce yoghurt into the diet; it's a great probiotic. But don't serve it cold. After 12 months old, the baby can be fed with whole wheat chapatis by soaking them in hot milk and jaggery. Once it's soft, it's ready to be enjoyed for breakfast.

Dhalia Kichidi for Babies

Ingredients:

Half cup roasted broken wheat

Half cup steamed veggies of your choice

1 cup of water

Pinch of salt

Pinch of turmeric

Preparation:

Add all the ingredients into a cooker and cook for 30 minutes. Mash it and serve.

Some Do's and Don'ts for Feeding Babies

Don't feed babies hurriedly. Let them eat at their own pace.

Don't feed biscuits and bread to the baby.

Don't feed raw veggies and fruits to the baby.

Keep an eye on their tongue. Clean them softly with your hands.

Massage the baby for better digestion.

Digestive Recipes

Not so long ago, there was a trend of infused water. Did you try them for the hype and supposed health benefits? Well, we all have been there. But the sad fact is detox water does not flush toxins off our body. But healthy eating habits from Ayurveda will surely help.

In Ayurveda toxin, it is called ama that occurs due to improperly digested food, weak digestion, and bad dietary habits. According to the Centre for Disease Control and Prevention, about 50 million Americans seek the help of doctors for digestive problems.

Ayurveda claims our health and wellbeing mostly depend on how well we can digest foods. Our lifestyle and food choices we make can affect our digestion. Here are some recipes for people with digestive problems.

CCF Tea

In Ayurveda, this miracle tea is hailed for its amazing benefits on the digestive system. CCF refers to cumin, coriander, and fennel tea. This tea aids in digestion, absorption, metabolism. Take this tea in a thermos and sip it all day. Add mint to it during summers.

Ingredients:

¼ teaspoon cumin seeds

6 cups of water

½ teaspoon fennel seeds

½ teaspoon coriander seeds

Preparation:

In a pot, boil all the ingredients. Then in low heat, boil for 10 minutes. Strain the seeds. And it's ready to sip.

Kanji or Rice Porridge

This popular dish from India is a go-to recipe when someone is sick. Even doctors highly recommend this in sickness and especially with digestive problems. It's mild-tasting, light, and easily digestible. This is consumed for breakfast or dinner in the southern part of India.

Ingredients:

½ cup basmati rice

1 tablespoon ghee

6 cups of water

1 teaspoon salt

1/2 tablespoon black pepper powder

Preparation:

In a large bowl of water, add rice and bring it to a boil. Reduce the heat to low and cover the pot for 3o minutes. Add the salt, pepper, and ghee and serve hot. For a sweeter and creamier version, replace the water with coconut milk or milk.

Sauerkraut

Although "sauerkraut" came from Germany, it originated in China and made its way to Europe during the days of the "great wall of china." did you know sauerkraut was the superfood behind reduced death rates during the

American civil war. Sauerkraut is rich in vitamin C, K, calcium, potassium, and phosphorous. It has dietary fiber. The healthy probiotics in it boost the immune system, help you digest well and lose weight, may prevent cancer, and improve brain function by reducing stress. We must try consuming this for all the goodness it offers.

Ingredients:

1/2 kg white cabbage (sliced)

1/2 kg red cabbage (sliced)

2 grated carrots

1 grated beetroot

1inch grated ginger

2 garlic cloves (minced)

1 tablespoon turmeric or 1-inch fresh grated turmeric root

3 tablespoon crystal sea salt

1 teaspoon caraway seeds

1 teaspoon peppercorns

Preparation:

1. In a large bowl, add in the cabbage and salt and massage for good 10 minutes until you see the liquid at the base of the bowl and cabbage as reduced a bit.

2. Now, let's add in the carrots, garlic, ginger, beetroot and turmeric and crushed pepper, and caraway seeds for immense flavor. Mix them all again.

3. Pack them into jars and let the liquid from cabbage rise above for optimum fermentation. The longer its fermented sourer cabbage gets. You can store it in the fridge for up to 6 months.

Rose Lassi

Lassi is a Punjabi drink made of yoghurt and sugar. To

give this traditional recipe a spin, we are adding rose petals to it. Roses are rich in vitamins C and A. If you don't have fresh rose flowers in your garden, you can replace them with rose water. You can find rose water in Asian or middle eastern sections in grocery stores. Give this pink flowery drink a try post-lunch in summers, and it will soothe your tummy and keep you hydrated.

Ingredients:

½ cup fresh homemade yoghurt

1 cup of water

1 pinch cardamom powder

1 rose flower petals or 1 tsp rose water

Jaggery or maple syrup to taste

Preparation:

Blend them all until smooth and have it. Yes, it's as

simple as that.

Fresh Cilantro Digestive Lassi

The herb cilantro is known for its digestive support. Cilantro activates and releases digestive enzymes and aid in better digestion. This lassi is best at preventing bloating, flatulence, nausea, indigestion, and also in absorbing the nutrients from food. Consume this lassi before lunch to ignite that much needed digestive fire.

Ingredients

3 cups of water (room temperature)

Pinch of rock salt

1 cup fresh homemade yoghurt

Pinch of black pepper powder

Pinch of dry roasted cumin seed powder

½ tsp. chopped cilantro leaves

Preparation:

Blend them all and serve them at room temperature. Fresh cilantro leaves works as a digestion booster. Makes digestion easy.

Jaggery Ginger Balls

We tend to overeat during Festivals and buffets; well, it all looks great until the agony of a stomach ache. Our mind goes through a million thoughts, and we end up in a panic. In Ayurveda, there's an antidote for stomach ache. That is these tiny jaggery ginger balls which work wonders when pain is due to indigestion and flatulence. The magic that these two ingredients do is bring in the digestive enzymes to action and cleanse the intestine.

Ingredients:

2 tablespoon grated dried ginger

7 tablespoons of grated palm jaggery

Preparation:

Combine both the ingredients in a small bowl and mix them. Now, make 12 equal portions and make them into 12 balls. Store them in an airtight container and consume them within a week.

Insomnia Recipes

Can't fall asleep? Neither can our 60 million fellow Americans, insomnia, and the demand for melatonin is at an all-time high. Well, melatonin is a hormone that puts us to sleep, and more and more people are dependent on this. It's so unfortunate that we need to be taught to sleep these days. Like we use a lullaby to put our babies to sleep, now we have calming apps and sound therapy to put us to sleep.

Insomnia is not only trouble falling asleep but also mid-sleep awakenings, like feeling awake 4 hours into night's sleep. In the long run sleep, deprivation can cause serious damage to the brain by overstimulating certain parts. It can accelerate brain damage due to Alzheimer's. Sleep medications are highly addictive, and on long-term use, they can hinder natural sleep and have major withdrawal symptoms; moreover, they are expensive. For all the bad things they can do to us. It's always safe to use herbal medicine for this. And Ayurveda exceptionally has some of the best remedies for all the night owls reading this. I have you some recipes that put us to sleep when consumed over some time at regular intervals.

Pumpkin Seed Butter

Pumpkin seeds are the source of an amino acid tryptophan that can promote sleep. You will need 1 gram of tryptophan to improve sleep. Pumpkin seeds are also a rich source of zinc and magnesium. Zinc helps in the conversion of tryptophan to serotonin (the happy hormone), which in turn converted to melatonin (sleep hormone). Magnesium levels are also linked with improved sleep quality, total sleep time. More the magnesium better the sleep. This butter can be stirred into soups and smoothies or as salad toppings.

Ingredients:

1 cup of pumpkin seeds

1 tablespoon raw honey

½ cup of sunflower seeds

2 tablespoon cinnamon powder

Pinch pink salt

Pinch of ground ginger

Pinch of turmeric

Preparation:

Soak both the seeds in water for 6 - 8 hours. Drain the water and pat dry the seeds on the towel. Put them in a blender add honey, ginger, cinnamon, salt. Blend them until creamy. Store this butter in an airtight jar.

Deep Sleep Tonic

Milk alone has high amounts of tryptophan and melatonin. According to Ayurveda, drinking milk before bed can put us to sleep. Nutmeg in this tonic has healing properties like calming and relaxing nerves and activates serotonin and melatonin, putting us to sleep. Use freshly grated nutmeg for deep sleep. Consume milk with a dash of nutmeg can improve sleep quality. Consume this deep sleep tonic an hour before bed for deep slumber sleep.

Ingredients:

10 soaked almonds

1 teaspoon ghee

1 cup whole milk

½ cup of water

3 - 4 pitted dates

½ teaspoon cinnamon powder

½ teaspoon cardamom powder

Dash of freshly grated nutmeg powder

Pinch of fresh black pepper powder

Pinch of turmeric

Preparation:

1. Soak almonds in water for 8 hours.

2. In a blender, add the almonds, dates, cinnamon, cardamom, ghee, milk, nutmeg, turmeric, pepper, and water and blend until they are liquefied for 2- 3 minutes.

3. In a saucepan, add this mixture and bring it to a boil and turn down the heat and remove from the pan. Serve it in a mug and drink it warm.

Khus Khus Doodh

As we all know, poppy seeds are effective in inducing sleep. They are known to calm the brain and bring down stress levels. Drink this warm milk one hour before sleep for a blessed slumber.

Ingredients:

2 tbsp white poppy seeds

2 - 3 cardamom pods

8 - 10 soaked almonds

Jaggery to taste

1 teaspoon turmeric powder

2 glass of milk

2 tablespoon ghee

Preparation:

1. Soak poppy seeds in water overnight.

2. In another bowl of water, soak almonds for 3-4 hours. Peel the skin off almonds.

3. Now, blend almonds and poppy seeds, some water into a smooth paste. Take this paste into a bowl.

4. In a saucepan, heat ghee, add the paste and stir over low heat. Cook and keep stirring for 10 - 15 minutes or until it's light brown.

5. Add the milk, turmeric, and cardamom powder. Stir and boil on high heat for once and turn down to low heat and cook uncovered for 10 minutes.

6. The sides of the pan might have thick cream, scrape this and add it to milk. Turn off the heat and add grated jaggery powder and mix well. Serve it warm.

Ashwagandha Sleep Tonic

The botanical name "Somnifera" is a Latin translation for 'sleep-inducing.' This miracle root is hailed for its effects on other parts of the body as well. It has been in use for centuries to relieve stress, anxiety and as an antidepressant and sleep inducer.

Ingredients:

One and a half cups of water

2 raw macadamia nuts

2 Medjool date

1/2 teaspoon cinnamon powder

2 pinches of nutmeg powder

Half a teaspoon of clove powder

Pinch of fine sea salt

1/2 vanilla bean or 2 drops on vanilla essence

1 teaspoon of ashwagandha root powder

Preparation:

1. Add all the ingredients, even the vanilla bean, without scraping the seeds out. Blend them till creamy.

2. In a pot, heat the mixture on low heat. Strain and serve in a glass and sprinkle some cinnamon.

Brazil Nut Cinnamon Milk

Brazil nuts are the richest sources of selenium. And selenium supplements are proven to help protect brain cells, improve mood and mental performance. Low selenium levels are linked to neurodegenerative changes and impacting our ability to fall asleep. This nutty milk makes you sleep like a baby.

Ingredients:

3 cups roasted Brazil nuts

1 vanilla bean or 1 tablespoon of vanilla extract

2 tablespoons of honey or maple syrup

1 tablespoon cinnamon powder

1 teaspoon of salt

1 teaspoon ghee

Preparation:

In a blender, add the roasted nuts, vanilla, cinnamon, honey, and salt. Blend them all and serve in a glass and add ghee. Enjoy!

Hair and Skin Recipes

Good skin and hair add up to a healthier and happier you. Those good hair days and great skin days are all we crave for each day. But to look good and to feel confident, you need to give the proteins and vitamins they need. Remember, your skin sheds dead cells every day. The great skin that you have today may not look the same tomorrow, instead of spending a fortune on the products which do not suit or work for all skin types. Eat foods that suit every skin. Did you know 60% of us use products that don't work and even might cause harm to your skin? That's called negative skincare.

And the worst thing is we are constantly influenced by the marketing strategies, opinions we never asked for and the fast-fashion selling us new products every week, millions of products that mostly don't work. We all know that beauty trends change like the wind. In 2020 they came up with vegan and cruelty-free, fragrance-free, inhalable beauty that has access to the nervous system and works on mind and skin simultaneously.

Not so long ago, we had sulfate and paraben-free, rice water trend for hair care, and currently, the argon oil and the funniest of all that happened in 2020 is microbiome movement, the beauty line that has prebiotics, probiotics, and postbiotics for scalp and body scrubs. I just can't stop laughing at this one. I'm not sure if they work or no, but you will surely benefit from consuming them. These trends might change what remains constant is the foods and natural benefits.

The food choices you make today will give you flawless skin 30 years from now. It's a lifelong process and lots of healthy food in every meal that it takes to develop great skin. I have some interesting antioxidant-rich recipes that are great for your skin and hair.

Amla Curry

If you ever wondered what makes India the largest exporter of human hair. The secret behind thick, lustrous hair even in their late 60s is the Ayurvedic fruit amla - Indian gooseberry. It's been an Indian woman's beauty treasure trove for ages. It is rich in vitamin C and antioxidants like tannins making it an anti-aging remedy, and you don't need those expensive anti-aging vitamin C serums. This recipe prevents premature greying and promotes healthy hair growth.

Ingredients:

1 cup chopped amla

2 slit green chilies

One and a half tablespoon mustard oil

1/2 teaspoon fennel seeds

1/2 teaspoon cumin seeds

1/2 teaspoon mustard seeds

1/2 teaspoon turmeric powder

1/2 teaspoon chili powder

1 teaspoon crushed coriander seeds

A few chopped coriander leaves

1/4 teaspoon hing

1 tablespoon jaggery

Salt to taste

Preparation:

1. In a pan, heat the mustard oil on low flame, add chilies, mustard seeds, cumin seeds.

2. Add in the amla and cook for 3 minutes on a medium flame.

3. Add turmeric, chili powder, hing, coriander, and fennel seeds, and cook for a minute.

4. Now, add the jaggery and 1/2 cup water and cook for 4 minutes while stirring. Garnish with coriander and serve hot with hot rice and ghee.

Avocado Chocolate Pudding

Avocado is great for hair and skin for the essential fatty acids, antioxidants, minerals, and Biotin it has. Biotin is a famous supplement used for hair loss. Avocado is known for increasing collagen metabolism by repairing the damage by UV rays. And cacao powder is rich in omega 6 fatty acids, antioxidants fight the free radicals.

Polyphenols in cacao reverse the signs of aging. The anti-cancerous properties of holy basil prevent skin cancer. Proanthocyanins in blueberries are known for improving skin texture. Do you need more reasons to try this recipe? Drink it twice or thrice a week for a goddess-like hair.

Ingredients:

1 avocado

1 teaspoon vanilla essence

Pinch of cardamom powder

2 tablespoons cacao powder

5 Blueberries for garnish

Holy basil for garnish

Jaggery or maple syrup

Salt

Preparation:

1. Scoop out the green flesh of the avocado into a blender.

2. Add in the cacao powder, cardamom, vanilla, jaggery, and salt and blend until smooth.

3. Serve it in a glass and garnish with blueberries and holy basil on top. Enjoy!

Green Smoothie

Spinach is a power-packed leaf that's loaded with folate, iron, vitamin A and C; all of these promote healthy hair growth and enhance the radiance of the skin. Vitamin A helps the skin heal from sun damage and scars. The grape seed extract has been in trend for a while now for its effective fight against free radicals and reduces oxidative stress.

The skin and pulp also possess equal benefits for skin and hair. They have flavonoids and antioxidants that revitalize skin help reduce blemishes, wrinkles, fine lines, and age spots. As we already know beta carotene in carrots prevent degeneration of cells and boost collagen growth.

Ingredients:

2 hands full of grapes with seeds

1 finely chopped carrot

2 hands full of spinach

125 ml of water

Preparation:

Add all ingredients and blend well. Drink straight away without straining. Enjoy at room temperature.

Antiaging Platter

Anti-aging skincare ranges are the most sought out products these days. At the age of 25, the signs of aging begin to appear. This platter is a gift from skin gods. This platter has powerful antioxidants to fight free radicals. Free radicals are the bad guys that accelerate the aging process and, through inflammation, cause breakouts, and skin issues.

Sprouts are rich in vitamin B, which regulates sebum production. Paneer is rich in selenium, antioxidants, and vitamin E. When it comes to curb aging, selenium is a key player. The high amount of citric acid in oranges exfoliates the skin from within and dry out acne, reverse wrinkles formation and premature aging. Dates prevent the accumulation of melanin and give you a bright skin tone.

Omega 3 fats in walnuts and Vitamin E in almonds improve elasticity and nourish your skin. And watermelon pumps hydration to your skin. So try this platter for breakfast once or twice a week.

Ingredients:

2 tablespoon sprouted green grams

1/4 cup paneer or tofu

1/4 teaspoon chili powder

1/4 teaspoon salt

1/4 teaspoon cumin powder

Pinch of turmeric

1/4 cup grapes with seeds

6 orange segments

2 dates

4 walnuts

5 almonds

1/2 cup watermelon

Preparation:

In a bowl, mix the sprouts, salt, paneer, cumin powder, turmeric, chili powder and mix them. Take a plate and arrange fruits and nuts on one side and sprouts and panner on another side. The anti-aging platter is ready to eat.

Lemon Ginger Chutney

Lemon, bright sunshine that lifts our skin as bright as the sun. Lemon has been long hailed for its skin lightening properties, age spots, and scars included. Its astringent qualities, the high pH levels reduce inflammation and oil production. The antifungal properties can kill fungus candida on the skin. Ginger evens out the skin tone, reduces cellulite, improves elasticity. And for the tresses, ginger increases the blood circulation to the scalp, which is essential in stimulating hair follicles. The vitamin E in olive oil improves the elasticity of the skin.

Ingredients:

2 tablespoons of grated fresh ginger

1 tablespoon of the fresh ginger juice from the grating process

1/4 cup fresh lemon juice

1 teaspoon jaggery or coconut sugar

1 tablespoon lemon zest

1 tablespoon of olive oil

Preparation:

In a bowl, add the ginger and its juice, jaggery, lemon juice, lemon zest, and olive oil. Store it in the refrigerator in an airtight jar. But remember to always serve at room temperature, or warm the jar by keeping it in hot water before serving.

Fruit Yoghurt Parfait

Is your skin prone to acne and unsightly blemishes? Are breakouts your constant friend? Is dull skin crushing your confidence and emotionally upsetting? Then this four berry yoghurt parfait is pumped up with Vitamin C and an abundance of antioxidants. As I mentioned earlier about probiotics being used as scalp and body scrubs, yoghurt is a probiotic that's got good microbes not only for your gut but to make your skin glow. It moisturizes the dull-looking skin, and lactic acid in it exfoliates the dead cells and leaves you with a new layer of skin.

Ingredients:

3 cups of vanilla yoghurt or coconut yoghurt

1 cup fresh strawberries and some strawberry juice

1 pint of blueberries, blackberries, raspberries

1 cup of granola

Preparation:

Layer some vanilla yoghurt into all 4 tall glasses at the bottom. Combine strawberries and their juice with fresh berries. Add Alternate layers of granola, fruit with yoghurt. Fill glasses. Serve them immediately to keep the granola crunchy.

Diabetic Recipes

America is home to 100 million diabetics, according to the Center for Disease Control. The burden of diabetes in Americans is enormous. 34.2 million Americans, that is, 1 in 10 are diabetics and 88 million adults in Americans, approximately 1 in 3 adults are prediabetics. This data is enough to tell us the magnitude of this disease.

Diabetes is a chronic disease but is manageable with lifestyle changes. It gives me immense pride to say that Ayurveda is the best-sought health system for diabetic care in India. And the results are incredible. Diabetes needs to be addressed due to its plethora of complications, which can be fatal. Diabetics are prone to complications if blood sugars are not controlled. Diabetes can reduce one's life span due to its complications like vision loss, heart diseases, kidney failure, stroke, gangrene, which leads to amputations of legs or toes and feet.

As per Ayurveda, treatment for diabetes goes beyond dietary habits and physical activity. Ayurveda believes stress aggravates this disease, so alongside eating these recipes, one needs to practice yoga and meditation.

Coconut Bitter Gourd Curry

In India, bitter gourd is consumed with combinations like grated coconut makes it very tasty. The humble bitter gourd is a great blood purifier and works amazingly for preventing and treating type 2 diabetes. Coconut meat is rich in proteins, and fiber makes it a good choice to combine it along with bitter gourd. So just cook it this Indian way to make it tasty and palatable. Eat it with chapatis, tortillas, or even along with warm rice and ghee.

Ingredients:

100 grams of grated coconut

3 bitter gourds

Pinch of turmeric

1 teaspoon mustard seeds

10 leaves curry leaves

2 teaspoon coconut oil

1 finely chopped onion

Salt to taste

1 teaspoon Indian garam masala

Preparation:

1. Scrape the outer coverings slightly of bitter gourds and

then chop them into long thin strips.

2. Heat a saucepan over medium heat and add the coconut oil; add the mustard seeds and let them pop. Now add in the curry leaves and onions, some salt.

3. Pinch of turmeric and fry the onions until slightly brown. Add the bitter gourd strips and cook them covered for 5 minutes or until tender.

4. Finally, add the Indian garam masala and shredded coconut at the end. Have it for lunch with chapatis or warm rice.

Diabetic Homemade Jam

For all those diabetics who love toast and jam, I have psyllium and fresh berry jam for you. Psyllium is derived from the Plantago ovate, an herb found in India. The seeds of this plant give us this soluble fiber psyllium. The resistance of psyllium for digestion allows it to reduce the blood sugars. It also aids in weight loss. It improves glycemic control in type 2 diabetes. You can find this husk in Indian stores. Psyllium acts like gelatin, and it takes just about 5 minutes to make this jam.

Ingredients:

1 cup of fresh Summer berries

1 tablespoon of fresh lemon juice

1 tablespoon psyllium husks

Pinch of pink Himalayan salt or mineral salt

Preparation:

In a blender, add the summer berries, lemon juice, salt, and psyllium husk and pulse them to get a chunky consistency. Spread this psyllium jam on toast or add it into smoothies, breakfast bowls or use to dress up cakes and desserts. Store this jam in an airtight jar, or you can refrigerate it and it up to a week.

Cilantro Pesto

Cilantro is popular among the Mexican, Indian, and Thai cuisines. It's valued for its cooling effects on our body. It also chelates toxic metals and helps tissues. Cilantro is long hailed for its ability in blood sugar management. It improves liver health and thereby reducing blood sugars. There is a belief that cilantro could be a remedy for diabetes. According to studies, Cilantro extract reduces the blood sugars in conditions like obesity and high blood sugars. The effects of cilantro were similar to *glibenclamide*, an anti-diabetic drug.

Ingredients:

1 bunch of cilantro

1 garlic clove

2 tablespoons of roasted pumpkin seeds

Lemon juice of 1 lemon

Salt to taste

Freshly crushed black pepper

Extra virgin olive oil

Preparation:

1. Rinse the bunch of cilantro. Pat dry the cilantro. Further, pluck the leaves and add them into a blender along with pumpkin seeds and garlic. Pulse them for a chunky consistency.

2. Now, add the lemon juice to the mixture. Pulse it again until you achieve pesto consistency. If you find pesto too dry, add some more lemon juice; if you find it runny, add more pumpkin seeds and blend. Adjust according to your taste.

3. Now, finally, season with some salt and pepper. Transfer the pesto into a bowl and drizzle some olive oil, and stir. Toss it with pasta or add it into soups. You can also enjoy it as a dip along with side sliced vegetables.

Stuffed Bitter Gourd

This baked bitter gourd stuffing is a healthy starter for diabetics. As I mentioned earlier about the benefits of eating bitter gourd, the bitterness of this vegetable works like an antidote for sugars in the body. This recipe from Kerala is eaten like kababs, and the Indian spices make these bitter bombs a yummy go-to snack for diabetics for tea time snack as well.

Ingredients:

5 small bitter gourds

200 grams of cottage cheese

2 sliced onions

2 tablespoon coconut oil

1 teaspoon cumin powder

1 teaspoon coriander powder

1 teaspoon red chili powder

Salt to taste

1/2 teaspoon jaggery

Preparation:

1. Scrape the outer skin of bitter gourds, now cut open them from the top. Now scoop out the core and the seeds of them. Keep them aside.

2. To prepare the filling. Heat the saucepan over medium heat and add the coconut oil; add the onions and sauté them till golden brown.

3. Now, to these sauteed onions, add the coriander powder, cumin powder and chili powder, and lastly, salt. To this, add half a teaspoon jaggery and crumbled cottage cheese.

4. Now, let's start the filling, take 1 tablespoon of this filing and fill this into bitter gourd shells.

5. Now, take a flat pan and oil the pan, and place the stuffed bitter gourds. Bake them at 325 degrees for 15 minutes. Remember to turn the bitter gourds in between to make sure they are cooked evenly.

Paneer Methi Chaman

Fenugreek is widely used in India for its various benefits. Fenugreek seeds contain fiber that slows down the digestion and absorption of sugars and carbohydrates. These seeds also help in altering the way our body uses sugar and increases insulin production. And usage of fenugreek flour also reduces insulin resistance. Alongside, that the spinach and cottage cheese and the ayurvedic spices make this recipe highly nutritious. Try this leafy, creamy recipe with hot chapatis.

Ingredients:

1 teaspoon Kasuri methi (dried fenugreek)

2 cups of chopped fresh fenugreek leaves

1 cup of cottage cheese

4 cups chopped spinach

2 tablespoons of coconut oil

1/4 cup of chopped onions

1 teaspoon cumin seeds

1/4 teaspoon chili powder

Pinch of turmeric powder

1/4 teaspoon asafetida

1 teaspoon chili-ginger paste

1/4 teaspoon coriander powder

1/4 teaspoon Indian garam masala.

Salt to taste

2 tablespoon unsalted butter.

Preparation:

1. In a pan over medium heat, roast the Kasuri methi till crisp and keep it aside.

2. Now, blanch the fenugreek and the spinach leaves in a pot of boiling water for 2minutes. Drain it.

3. In a blender, blend them smooth and set it aside.

4. Heat a saucepan over medium heat and add the coconut oil, cumin seeds, onions and sauté them till they turn translucent.

5. Now, add the asafetida, chili powder, turmeric powder, coriander powder, and chili-ginger paste and sauté for few seconds.

6. Add the green leaf puree and sauté for 3 minutes.

7. Finally, add the salt, garam masala, cottage cheese, and cook for 2-3 minutes on medium heat. Turn off the heat and add the butter. Serve hot with chapati.

Detox Spice Tadka

Although we are in an era of modern medicine and insulin became a boon to all diabetics. We often tend to forget that nature offers us a lot. Our food is our medicine, and the solution to most of the issues lies in our kitchen. Did you know turmeric is a natural anti-diabetic, and it helps with insulin resistance, in turn allowing the glucose to enter the cells efficiently?

Coriander seeds, on the other hand, keep a check on blood sugars. And the tiny Cumin seeds not only manage blood sugars but also curbs weight gain and maintains a healthy weight. Excess weight is one of the major culprits that make us diabetic. This spice mix is an excellent remedy to combat the sugars in our body.

Ingredients:

1 spoon of turmeric powder

1 teaspoon of turmeric

2 teaspoons spoons of ground cumin powder

3 teaspoons of spoons ground coriander powder

4 spoons of ground fennel powder.

2 tablespoons of ghee

Chopped vegetables of your choice

Preparation:

1. In a jar, add all the spices and mix them well.

2. While you cook a meal, in a frying pan over low heat, add some amount of ghee and add the spice mix. Sauté the spices till the aroma lasts; it would take 1-2 minutes.

3. Make sure not to burn the spices. Now add salt and black pepper to it, now add your favorite veggies and sauté them for a minute more.

Yoghurt Dill Dip

This dip tastes delicious with hot chapatis or with

tortillas. Dill leaves are known for their antidiabetic and antioxidant properties. Consuming dill leaf can calm down our insulin fluctuations and control the blood sugars. The antioxidants in dill leaves are known for preventing metabolic disorders like diabetes. Moreover, the dill leaf is also known for controlling the thyroid functions and boost our immunity. You can also simply use this dip as a salad dressing or as a dip along with fresh vegetables. Thin it with olive oil

Ingredients:

1 bunch of dill

1 teaspoon of mayonnaise

1 cup of plain homemade yoghurt

Juice of 1 lemon

Salt to taste

Freshly crushed black pepper

Preparation:

Rinse the bunch of dill and finely chop them. Now take a medium bowl and add the dill into the bowl. Add in the mayonnaise, lime juice, and yoghurt. Whisk them properly; finally, add the salt and pepper to it and mix well. You can also replace yoghurt with cottage cheese.

Neem Juice

The first thing that comes to our mind when the thought of neem is its extreme bitterness. But if that bitterness can save us from diabetes, then why not try it? Neem tree has been the best friend for ancient Indians and Ayurvedic practitioners. Neem juice works great as an antidiabetic tonic. It also boosts metabolism and aids in weight loss. It's difficult to chew the leaves due to the bitter taste. It's easy to have tiny shots of this juice.

Ingredients:

1 cup of fresh neem leaves

1/2 cup water

Preparation:

In a blender, add the neem leaves and water and blend them well. Now, strain the mixture. Serve the neem juice immediately. Drink this juice once you wake up on an empty stomach. Ayurveda suggests not to consume anything half an hour after having this juice.

Weight Loss Recipes

Are you someone who gains weight just by watching someone eat? Did you try all those fad diets and tired of them? Are you frustrated with your non-existing or merely existing metabolism? Do you suffer from PCOD, thyroid, depression, or anything that makes you put on kilos? Well, According to the CDC, Americans are eating more calories than they did before.

The size of the obesity epidemic in America has constantly been growing. And the manipulative marketing strategies of the food and diet industry influencing our dietary habits. Left us all confused between diet and nutrition. After all, those fancy commercials are selling us the idea that eating junk is cool. The diet industry in the US grew faster, bigger, and smarter. It's hard for this generation to escape from processed foods, drive-thru meals, fast foods, and large portions.

On the other hand, there is a rise in people opting for weight loss schemes, fad diets, weight loss supplements, and finally, bariatric surgeries. We are looking for fast foods as well as fast weight loss schemes. Let us not lose sight of the bigger picture here; over the decade, many fad diets have come and gone. We dint stop rushing to blame the foods like gluten, sugar, fat, dairy. We have gone free of all of them. But what change did it make? It just made the diet industry some profits. Soon, the fat-free, sugar-free, gluten-free products flooded the shelves of supermarkets. It took us years to figure out that; how come food that's free of all these was still so flavorful?

Isn't it too good to be true?! With the increase in obesity, diseases like diabetes, coronary artery diseases, cancer, and stroke also increased. It is estimated that Obesity is linked to approximately 60 chronic diseases. Along with the horrible foods around us, lack of physical activity is a major culprit too. Now more and more people are choosing Ayurveda for losing weight.

As I have mentioned earlier, Ayurveda is a way of living and not just a health science. The age-old Ayurveda left us with some weight loss recipes that give promising results. Allow yourself to believe in ayurvedic eating and stay healthy and fit with these recipes.

Coconut Mint Chutney

This coconut meat recipe promotes weight loss. But how? Thanks to the keto revolution for making MCT's so famous. The MCT's in this fruit gives us a feeling of heaviness on the stomach and further shed calories and burn fat. The fiber-rich coconut meat keeps us full for a longer time and keeps our hunger cravings at bay, and prevents us from binge eating. Our cool mint leaves is a metabolism booster, it activates the digestive enzymes that help in better absorption of nutrients.

When nutrients are assimilated properly, our metabolism spikes up, and as we all know, the faster the metabolism, the thinner the bodies. Swap those high-fat creamy dips with this Ayurvedic coconut mint chutney. I call this Ayurvedic keto dip. In India, this chutney is a staple among south Indians. It is cooked at-least thrice a week as snack time or breakfast dip with idli and dosa. This makes a great salad dip, just add some thinned olive oil and enjoy!

Ingredients:

Half cup shredded coconut

One and a half inch fresh ginger

¼ teaspoon salt

1 tablespoon of warm water

Pinch of turmeric

2 bunches of fresh mint leaves

1 teaspoon of coconut oil

1 teaspoon brown mustard seeds

1 tablespoon of fresh lime juice

Preparation:

1. In a blender, add the shredded coconut, water, ginger, turmeric, lime juice, and mint leaves, and pulse them to blend. Transfer this into a small bowl.

2. Now, take a saucepan and warm the coconut oil over medium heat. Add the brown mustard seeds and let the mustard seeds pop.

Then turn off the heat and remove the pan from heat and add the mustard seeds and oil to the coconut chutney and stir well and serve.

Steamed Spicy Veggies

This recipe is extremely low in calories, made with keto-friendly veggies like cauliflower and broccoli; cauliflower is rich in fiber and makes our digestion slow as a snail. Since it's made up of 90 % water, it is weight loss-friendly and keeps us full for a longer time.

Broccoli, on the other hand, is a good carb with a high amount of fiber. Again, making the digestion a lengthy process. Arugula is a low-calorie leaf; 20 grams of arugula has just 5 calories. That's the least amount of calories any veggie could have. This fiber-rich recipe keeps us full for a long and far away from munching on food.

Ingredients:

2 cups of cauliflower florets

2 cups of broccoli florets

1/4 cup of pumpkin seeds

1 cup of arugula

1 tablespoon of finely chopped ginger

1 tablespoon of mustard oil

2 finely chopped garlic cloves

1 tablespoon of turmeric

2 teaspoons of coriander powder

2 tablespoons of mustard seeds

1 teaspoon of cardamom powder

Preparation:

1. In a large saucepan, warm the mustard oil and sauté the garlic, ginger, turmeric, cardamom, mustard seeds, and coriander. Stir frequently for a minute or two or until fragrant.

2. Now, add in the broccoli and cauliflower florets. Add little water and cover the pan; simmer until vegetables are soft; it takes about 5 minutes.

3. Add in the arugula and cook for another minute or until it's wilted. Serve with cooked barley and top with the pumpkin seeds.

Cucumber Raitha

Raitha is a staple side dish in Indian cuisine. Raita is

consumed alone or along with pulao. Cucumbers have just 45 calories and 90 percent water. Bone up on this calcium-rich yoghurt. Studies show that people who included fat-free yoghurt in their diet lost more calories. Moreover, we don't want dull-looking skin while we are on a diet, right? Yoghurt keeps your skin glowing while you lose weight. Enjoy this raitha whenever your cravings kick in or along with the salad. Ayurveda believes in consuming the skin of vegetables and fruits; they heal and nourish our skin. So, use cucumbers along with peels and enjoy.

Ingredients:

2 unpeeled Persian cucumbers

1 cup plain yoghurt

1 shredded carrot

Pinch of salt

Pinch of pepper

1 chopped cilantro

1 teaspoon of ground ginger

Preparation:

Cut the cucumbers lengthwise and slice them into thin quarter moons. Take a bowl, add the cucumbers, yoghurt, carrots, cilantro, and ginger. Add the salt and pepper for seasoning and mix well.

Zingy Green Smoothie

Kale is a low energy density leafy green. One cup of kale contains 4 grams of fiber, making it a great hunger suppressor. If you are suffering from a fatty liver, then the sulfur compounds in kale is an excellent detoxifier and promote liver health. Root ginger contains gingerols, which have effects on the biological activity of the body. Gingerols also have anti-obesity effects, anti-diabetic effects. Alongside, they speed up the process of digestion. Additional to these, celery is a fiber-rich stick that has only 10 calories. The pectin fiber in lemons keeps you full for a longer time. All these combined makes this fresh, zingy green smoothie a great fat burner.

Ingredients:

2 bunches of kale

A thin slice of root ginger

Half a stick of celery

100 ml of room temperature water

1 sweet apple

2 tablespoons of lemon juice

Half a cucumber

Preparation:

Chop the apple and cucumber into slices. In a blender, add the kale, celery, sliced ginger, and water and blend well. Add the chopped apple, cucumber, lemon juice, and blend well. Drink straight away at room temperature.

Asparagus Mushroom Medley

These lanky sticks can be your great friend for the weight loss journey. Asparagus contains a chemical called asparagine; this alkaloid acts straightaway on the cells and breaks down fats. Asparagine also increases insulin sensitivity, which helps our body store the energy in muscle instead of storing it as fat.

Asparagus contains a high amount of fiber, a lot of water and are low in calories. Mushrooms are tiny fungi bulbs that are rich in proteins. Both of these veggies boost our metabolism and aid in weight loss. Crunchy roasted asparagus and mushy mushrooms make a good dinner time meal during your weight loss journey.

Ingredients:

1 cup of chopped Asparagus

3/4 cup of sliced Mushrooms

1/4 cup of chopped red onion

1 sprig of fresh minced rosemary

1 tablespoon of olive oil

1 tablespoon of lemon juice

Pinch of turmeric

Pinch of salt

Pinch of fresh ground pepper

Preparation:

Preheat the oven to 450 F. In a bowl, add in the
asparagus, mushrooms, onions, and minced rosemary,
and drizzle the olive oil, salt, turmeric, crushed
peppercorns, and lemon juice. On a cookie sheet, spread
them into a thin layer. Roast them for 15- 20 minutes or
until the asparagus is tender. Serve them warm.

Carom and Cumin Seed Water

This metabolic booster tonic has two miracle ingredients; one is the carom seeds that contain thymol, which helps in the secretion of gastric juices that boost digestion and improve bowel movements; carom seeds are excellent natural laxatives and reduce water storage in the body aiding in weight loss. The cumin seeds activate enzymes that breakdown carbohydrates, sugars, and fats. After all, a good digestive system is the sole reason behind losing weight because, in turn, it boosts metabolism. And I need not mention fast metabolism. Simply boost the metabolism, and you will see shedding the extra fat even while sitting. This recipe does exactly that.

Ingredients:

25 grams of carom Seeds

25 grams of cumin Seeds

Water

Honey

Preparation:

In a glass of water, add in the carom seeds, followed by cumin seeds. Let the seeds soak in the water overnight. The next morning, stir the seeds and strain them. If needed, add a tablespoon of honey for taste.

Make a habit of drinking this first thing in the morning. Every day morning on an empty stomach, drink one glass of this drink. Try this at least for one month to see visible results of weight loss. Follow the rule of four weeks on and one week off. After using it for one month, take a 1-week break and start drinking it again.

Bitterest of All

This one is an ultimate weapon from our kitchen that aids in weight loss. Bitter gourd is a low calorie, fiber-rich vegetable. The fiber in this vegetable curbs the appetite and keeps you full for a longer time. Fiber is crucial for losing weight. Fiber-rich foods are hard on our digestive system and need more calories in order to be digested. They help burn belly fat and prevent bloating. This juice keeps our insulin levels in check. To manage our weight, it is essential to keep blood sugars at normal. This juice activates the hormone insulin, in turn preventing the storage of sugars as fat in our body. Overall, ultimately leading to weight loss.

Ingredients:

One peeled bitter gourd

One lemon

Pinch of salt

Preparation:

Take peeled bitter gourd and cut it into two halves from the center. Now scoop out the seeds and white flesh from bitter gourd. Now take the bitter gourd and chop them into small pieces and soak them in water for about 30 minutes. In a juicer, put the pieces of bitter gourd and add lemon juice and half teaspoon salt. Now blend them all to make a juice. Blend until it has reached fine consistency. Pour it into a glass and drink it on an empty stomach in the morning, preferably after your workout.

Include this drink in your weight loss regime. Another method of making it for the ones who can't bear the bitterness of this juice is by adding fruits that are low in glycemic index and rich in fiber.

Mental Health Recipes

Among all the mental health issues we humans suffer from, depression tops the list, with more than 264 million people suffering from it worldwide. Depression is not the usual mood swings and short span emotional responses to everyday challenges. It's way beyond that. When depression lasts for a longer period, even with moderate intensity, it may turn out as a serious health condition; in worst cases, it can also lead to suicide. Approximately 800,000 people commit suicide each year around the world. Even successful people couldn't escape from it as well.

Robin Williams, Chester Bennington, Avicii, Kate spade fell prey to depression. We witnessed a giant leap of awareness through the recent Oscar winner, "Joker." It was a massive hit because we could relate to the beautiful portrayal of mental illness. Mental illness remains to be shrouded in stigma and is constantly underrated. I want you to have the wisdom of foods that work as natural antidepressants.

Foods that are rich in omega 3 fatty acids, selenium, magnesium, antioxidants, probiotics, zinc, vitamin D, flavonoids have a great impact on mental health. Selenium deficiency is known to cause depression, and supplementation of selenium is known to improve mood.

The food sources that are rich in selenium are seafood, grains, eggs, yoghurt, cottage cheese—vegetables like carrots, potatoes, garlic, spinach, lentils, green peas, and lettuce. Brazil nuts are extremely rich in selenium. One whole brazil nut has 96 mcg of selenium. These recipes, when consumed over time, will surely help you. Along with this, try to go for yoga and meditation sessions.

Ginger Carrot Soup

Ginger carrot soup is one good bowl of radiance the vitamins A, D, E to strengthen our eyesight, which we all know, but the beta-carotene in carrots is a powerful antioxidant. Studies proved that people with higher levels of carotenoids were less likely to face depression. Selenium keeps our mood bright. Ginger can influence the happy hormone- serotonin and works as a natural anti-depressant and reduce anxiety.

Since ancient times, nutmeg has been used as a brain tonic; it has a "myristicin," a natural compound that keeps our brain sharp and increases focus. Nutmeg, on the other side, is known to reduce anxiety and induce sleep. Nutmeg is well sought among all-natural antidepressants; however, nutmeg should be taken moderately due to its side effects. Anything in moderation is healthy. Enjoy this satiating soup as a snack or for dinner to calm your mind and fall into deep slumber sleep.

Ingredients:

2 tablespoons of ghee

1-inch of fresh, roughly chopped ginger

1/2 teaspoon of ground ginger

1/2 teaspoon of ground fenugreek

1/2 teaspoon of ground cinnamon

1 teaspoon ground cardamom

1/2 teaspoon grated nutmeg

6 chopped carrots

1 teaspoon of lemon zest

4 cups of vegetable broth

Olive oil for drizzling

Any of 2 seasonal herbs, like basil, rosemary, or thyme for garnish

Preparation:

1. In a large soup pot, melt the ghee over medium heat. Stir in the cinnamon, nutmeg, cardamom, fenugreek,

dried ginger powder, and fresh chopped ginger and sauté for a minute.

2. Add in the vegetable broth, carrots, and boil. Turn down the heat to low, simmer for 10 minutes.

3. Take a blender and transfer the soup and blend to make a puree. Now return this soup to the soup pot and cook for another minute.

4. Serve in soup bowls and sprinkle the lemon zest and drizzle the olive oil and add your favorite herbs.

Pistachio Truffles

Pistachios are probably the most vitamin B6 rich foods around. They produce the finest gamma wave response, which is essential for cognitive processing, retaining information, healing, learning and imagination, and other key functions of the brain. They can strengthen the brain wave frequencies. Snacking pistachios in between work helped people focus on their work and increased productivity. The blended pistachios for these truffles will melt in your mouth and, by the end, give you crunchy sweet, delicious truffles. You can add your favorite toppings or add the mix of pistachio, basil, and orange topping with shredded coconut, cocoa powder, cardamom, and cinnamon powder.

Ingredients:

¾ cup of raw unsalted, divided pistachios

3 or 4 basil leaves

1 tablespoon orange zest

2 tablespoon freshly squeezed orange juice

Pinch of ground ginger

Pinch of ground fenugreek

Pinch of ground cinnamon

Pinch of ground cardamom

Pinch of grated nutmeg

4 pitted and roughly chopped Medjool dates

4 teaspoons coconut oil, divided, plus additional for rolling the dough

Salt for taste

Preparation:

1. In a small bowl, soak the 2/4 cup of pistachios in water for about 10 minutes. Drain them and rinse under cold water, pat dry on a towel.

2. Heat the pan over medium heat and add the leftover 1/4 cup of pistachios and toast them for 5 minutes. Stir and toss occasionally.

3. Transfer these toasted pistachios into a blender. Add in the basil and orange zest and pulse it to get a chunky blend for a few minutes. Transfer the mixture into a small bowl.

4. In a blender, add the soaked pistachios, dates, 1 teaspoon of pure coconut oil, a pinch of these spices - nutmeg, cardamom, ground ginger, fenugreek, cinnamon, orange juice, and salt. Blend until you achieve a smooth consistency. If you feel that mixture is dry, add more orange juice and blend it. Drizzle some maple syrup. Taste it and adjust the seasonings, like salt and sweet, or by adding spices.

5. It's easy to roll them into balls by refrigerating the dough for 15 minutes or up to 24 hours. Take some coconut oil and oil your hands into making a ball. Roll a small portion of dough to make balls. Repeat until the entire dough is rolled into balls.

6. Now roll all these dough balls in pistachio, basil, and orange topping and place them on a serving plate. You can serve them immediately or refrigerate them by storing them in an airtight container.

Bahrami Pesto

Bahrami is a miracle ayurvedic herb that is long hailed for its mental benefits. Bahrami is used by ayurvedic practitioners for ages for a plethora of benefits it has to offer. It is found to be effective as a stress buster and relieve anxiety, and as neuroprotective in Alzheimer's disease, and improved memory. Bahrami, when taken at bedtime, induces sleep. Bahrami has anti-epileptic properties as well. In India, kids are often fed with 2-3 raw leaves per day by their moms to improve brain function, which is, in fact, true. Kids tend to eat, thinking they could perform well in exams and get better grades. Enjoy this Ayurvedic Bahrami pesto like you do the basil pesto.

Ingredients:

1/2 cup olive oil

1/2 teaspoon grated fresh ginger

1 teaspoon finely ground black pepper

1 teaspoon salt

1/2 cup finely chopped pecans

1/4 teaspoon fennel powder

1/2 teaspoon coriander powder

1/2 cup chopped fresh tulsi basil

3 cups chopped curly kale

1/2 cup chopped fresh bhrami or 1/4 cup Bahrami powder

1 small, mashed avocado

1 tablespoon fresh lime juice

Preparation:

1. Warm some olive oil and add the fresh ginger, salt, black pepper, and pecans. Simmer until the aroma lasts, and add in the fennel, coriander, and basil.

2. Simmer for a minute more, then add in fresh bhrami leaves. Drizzle some water and cover the lid and simmer until the kale is soft. Remove from heat and let cool.

3. Blend the avocado and lime juice along with the remaining olive oil to make a smooth consistency. Serve on pearl barley or rice, or along with fresh pasta and vegetables.

You will be left with a delicious tasting pesto along with mental clarity. Bahrami is known to improve memory, rejuvenate the mind, improve concentration, and consciousness.

Barley Soup

Did you know carbs keep us happy? Yes, they do carbs boost our brain with the hormone serotonin, aka the happy hormone. Which makes us happy and relaxed. And the fact is that carbs also hasten sleep. Carbs also release tryptophan, an essential amino acid that makes serotonin and melatonin (sleep hormone). So, barley is the smart carbohydrate that is rich in soluble fiber. And the best source of healthy carbohydrates for mental health. This is a basic recipe; you can add any manner of your favorite vegetables to it. Pearl barley thickens and gives it a nice consistency. If you like hull-less barley, then cook for 30 minutes more.

Ingredients:

2 tablespoons of ghee

¼ cup of minced fresh parsley

Pinch of asafetida

1/4 teaspoon rosemary

1/2 bell pepper, chopped

1/2 teaspoon dried basil

1 stalk celery, thinly sliced

5 cups flavorful vegetable broth

1 carrot, grated

1/4 cup pearl barley

2 bay leaves

Fresh ground black pepper

Salt

Preparation:

1. In a soup pot, melt the ghee and add the asafetida, basil, rosemary, parsley, celery, bell pepper, and carrot. Sauté them for 5 minutes over low heat and keep stirring.

2. Add in the broth, bay leaves and barley, bring it to boil. Cover it and simmer for 1 to 1 1/2 hours or until barley is tender. Stir occasionally. Add the salt and pepper. Serve hot.

Sweet Potato Jackets

In India, I lived in Chennai for 4 years, where every weekend I visited Marina Beach, where beach vendors sell baked sweet potatoes marinated in a spice mix and stuffed with fillings of our choice; they called them jackets. I asked the vendor about the recipe, and she was happy enough to tell me. And since then, I have been making this recipe once in a while. Sweet potatoes are mood boosters loaded with magnesium and Vitamin B6; they activate the enzymes and mood-regulating neurotransmitters and thereby releasing dopamine. Enjoy these jackets for breakfast or snacks, along with a cup of Indian masala chai.

Ingredients:

2 scrubbed sweet potatoes

1/4 cup of plain whole yoghurt

2 tablespoon ghee

pinch of ground ginger

Pinch of ground fenugreek

Pinch of ground cinnamon

Salt for seasoning

Pinch of ground cardamom

Pinch of grated nutmeg

Fresh ground black pepper powder, for seasoning

2 tablespoons of chopped dill

Preparation:

1. Warm-up the oven to 475°F. In a baking dish, melt the ghee and add in the cardamom powder, grated nutmeg, fenugreek powder, cinnamon powder, and ground ginger.

2. Now roll the potatoes in the salt, ghee, spices and coat them well. Roast them for 45 minutes.

3. To check if it is cooked adequately, slide a knife through the center of the sweet potatoes, and it should slide easily.

4. Let it cool for some time, then slice them lengthwise, add more ghee, and season with pepper and salt. Spoon in the yoghurt to the center of sweet potatoes and sprinkle the dill.

Brazil Nut Cocoa Balls

Brazil nuts are rich in selenium and ellagic acids, which play a major role in brain health. Ellagic acid, a polyphenol that has protective and antidepressant effects on our brain. Low selenium levels are linked to neurodegenerative disorders like Parkinson's and Alzheimer's.

A study on mental impairment in older adults found that consuming one nut per day showed improved mental function and verbal fluency. Consuming cocoa or dark chocolate can help relieve anxiety and improve the symptoms of depression. People who consumed pure cocoa twice daily had a 70 % reduction in depressive symptoms. Need I say more? Reap the benefits of both Brazil nut and cocoa with these mood-enhancing tiny balls.

Ingredients:

1/2 cup brazil nuts

1 teaspoon cocoa nibs

2 tablespoon cocoa powder (unsweetened)

1 teaspoon coconut oil

Desiccated coconut

Pinch of salt

1 teaspoon maple syrup or honey

Preparation:

1. In a mixer, blend the Brazilian nuts till coarse.

2. Now take a deep bowl and add in the Brazil nut powder, cocoa nibs, cocoa powder pinch of salt and mix them well, then add in the coconut oil, maple syrup and mix them well.

3. Now divide this mixture into 12 equal portions to make balls. Roll each portion into small balls.

4. In a bowl of desiccated coconut, roll them on all sides

until they are evenly coated. Store them in an airtight container.

These nutty balls make a good snack time meal. I store them in a glass jar on my table in the living room and grab a ball when hungry.

Complete Well-Being Recipes

What is health? Health is a state of physical, mental, and social well-being and not just the absence of disease. We might be healthy physically but unhappy and sad mentally. But both the physical and mental state of us is what leads to complete well being; they are clearly interlinked. And along with this comes social well-being and emotional well being which means being happy, feeling good, and being able to have a positive outlook towards life with optimistic emotions; to be able to love and have compassion and being satisfied with life.

Well, the above-mentioned state of equilibrium is hard to achieve in this hurry-scurry life. But to some extinct, these recipes will help you. After all, food is medicine, and our life runs on food. Try out these power-packed recipes, which I call all-rounder foods that have an abundance of proteins and nutrients.

Roasted Root Ecrasse

Ecrasse is a French word for mash. Roasted root ecrasse is a healthier substitute for mashed potatoes. In this recipe, carrots, rutabagas, and turnips are all roasted and mashed along with Ayurvedic spices. It is delicious, like any good mash, and is seasoned simply with salt and crushed black pepper. Add this on top of salads or burritos, and enjoy!

Ingredients:

1 cup of rutabagas

1 cup of turnips

1 cup of carrots

1 tablespoon of ghee

Pinch of ground fenugreek

Pinch of ground cinnamon

Pinch of ground ginger

Pinch of turmeric

Pinch of ground cardamom

Pinch of freshly grated nutmeg

Pinch of freshly ground black pepper

1 cup of homemade coconut milk

Salt for seasoning

Preparation:

1. Warm up the oven to 475°F. With the help of a fork, prick the vegetables to make steam holes and place them on a baking dish.

2. Roast them for 45 minutes. To check if they are evenly cooked knife should slide through easily.

3. Now, take them out of the oven and let them cool for 5 minutes. Peel the vegetables.

4. Now, take a blender and add these peeled vegetables along with ghee, spices, and coconut milk. Blend until you achieve a creamy consistency. Finally, season it with salt and pepper.

Biryani

Although biryani is a Persian dish, biryani is the most

loved dish among Indians. The fondness of this dish among Indians is incredible. Every Indian state and culture has created its biryani. Biryani is made with aromatic rice and is a dish that's rich in spices and flavors. Biryani is the most searched food on google India due to its evolving flavors. Indians don't want to miss any of its kinds. Biryani is the most ordered food as well; Indians ordered 95 biryanis per minute in 2019. Let me be honest, biryani is not overrated, and you are just one try away from being its fan. Although biryani is cooked with meat, here, let's try vegetable biryani.

Ingredients:

1 cup of basmati rice

5 tablespoons of ghee

1 teaspoon turmeric powder

1 tablespoon of coriander powder

1 teaspoon cumin powder

1 cup of mint leaves

4 cloves

4 cinnamon sticks

1 tablespoon ginger garlic paste

2 cardamom pods

2 cups of boiling water

2 bay leaves

4 carrots cut into half-moons

½ cup of raisins

2 cups of chopped carrots

2 cups of potatoes

2 cups of chopped green beans

½ cup of cashew pieces

Preparation:

1. Soak the basmati rice for 30 minutes in water. Drain the water and set it aside.

2. Heat the pot on medium heat and melt 4 tablespoons of ghee. Add in the cinnamon sticks, cloves, cardamom pods and sauté for a minute.

3. Add the ginger garlic paste and stir it for a minute. Now add in the cumin powder and coriander powder, and mint leaves.

4. Add the green beans, carrots, potatoes, basmati rice cook for 2-3 minutes. Add water to it. Cover the lid and bring it to a boil. Turn down the heat to low and cook for 10 minutes.

5. Take a small pan and add 1 tablespoon of ghee. Add the cashews and fry them till golden. Add the raisins and sauté them until plump. Add these raisins into the biryani pot and serve warm.

Pho Soup

Pho soup is a national dish of Vietnam. It's popular street food in Vietnam; the reason I have included this here is, it marries the Ayurvedic six tastes into one scrumptious, healthy bowl. This soup is made of Buckwheat soba or rice noodles. And the Korean staple Kimchi, a fermented vegetable pickle like sauerkraut, or you can simply add sauerkraut or cucumber pickle. The point here is to get the probiotic bacteria through fermented foods. Bok choy's folate, vitamin A, vitamin C, and B6, potassium, dietary fiber paired with lack of cholesterol, green grams, and tofu makes this soup a great healthy choice for light dinner.

Ingredients:

2 cups of vegetable broth

2 cups of cooked rice noodles

1 head of Bok choy

Pinch of turmeric

Ground black pepper powder

Salt to taste

Pinch of asafetida

2 cups of green gram sprouts

1 cup of kimchi

2 tablespoon lime juice

A cup of tofu, cubed

Basil sprigs

Preparation:

In a soup pot, boil the broth. Separate the Bok choy leaves from the stem and add them to the broth and boil for 2 minutes. Add in the noodles and cook for a minute. Add the salt and pepper. Serve the soup into bowls and add the kimchi, and top with lime juice and sprouts. Finally, add cubed tofu and garnish with basil sprigs.

Borscht

Borscht is a soul food among eastern Europe with fermented vegetables that aid in digestion and nutritious roots that keep their vitality. The alternate flavors like sweet and sour give this soup a deep flavor. Traditional borscht calls for adding the sauerkraut and is cooked along with the soup. Ayurveda believes in adding sauerkraut as topping in the soup bowls to keep those good microbes and health benefits intact.

Ingredients:

4 beets

1 small, sweet potato

1/2 inch of minced fresh ginger

Pinch of ground ginger

Pinch of ground cinnamon

2 tablespoons of ghee

Pinch of turmeric

Pinch of ground fenugreek

Pinch of ground cloves

4 cups of vegetable broth

Salt for taste

Freshly crushed black pepper

½ cup of sauerkraut along with juices

Preparation:

1. Preheat the oven up to 450°F. Trim away the greens of beets, but keep the tops, stems, and tails intact to hold their flavored juices while they roast.

2. Scrub the sweet potato and beets. With the help of a

fork, pierce the holes into a sweet potato; these are steam holes. Brush some ghee on to sweet potato and beets. Now sprinkle some salt.

4. Place them on a baking dish and roast them for about 45 minutes or let the knife slide easily into them to check if they are properly cooked.

5. Remove and let them cool, peel them, and cut them into small pieces. In a large pot, melt the rest of the ghee on medium heat. Add in the ginger and spices. Stir them.

6. Now add in the sweet potato, beets, and broth. Bring them to a boil. Reduce the heat and cook for 10 more minutes.

7. In a blender, transfer one-quarter of the soup and blend to make a puree. Add this back to the pot and warm for a minute.

Turn off the heat and remove the pot from heat, and cool for 3 minutes. Add salt and pepper for seasoning. In a serving, bowls divide the soup and serve with a spoonful of sauerkraut.

Kitchari

The first thing that comes to mind when it comes to Ayurvedic eating is kitchari. When looking for Ayurveda, you will find kitchari in almost every reference. It is popular among beginners and longtime Ayurvedic practitioners. This staple is so famous that I'm bored of writing this recipe. However, this Ayurvedic staple has my heart, and I want my dear readers to try this. It's easily digestible and can be fed to all ages; it's cleansing, detoxifying, and balancing. Try this for breakfast or dinner.

Ingredients:

1 cup of basmati rice

1 tablespoon ghee

1 cup split green grams

4 cups of homemade vegetable broth

1 cup of chopped vegetables, such as broccoli, carrots,

celery, kale, or cauliflower

2 cups of water

2 tablespoons of sesame seeds

1 tablespoon mustard seeds

Salt to taste

1/2 tablespoons ground ginger

Freshly crushed black pepper

1/2 teaspoon ground cloves

1 teaspoon ground turmeric

1/2 teaspoon ground fenugreek

Fresh herbs like basil, thyme, or rosemary for garnishing

1 teaspoon shoyu or tamari

Preparation:

1. Wash the rice and green beans in water and drain them, and set them aside.

2. In a large pot, melt the ghee over medium heat. Add in the spices like ground ginger, turmeric, black pepper powder, ground clove powder, fenugreek powder, and salt.

3. Now add the mung beans and rice and mix them well to coat the spice and ghee blend.

4. Add the water and broth and bring them to boil. Now, reduce the heat and mix them well and cover the pot and cook for 20 minutes in low heat.

5. Now open the lid and add vegetables on top of the rice and green gram mixture. Cover the lid and cook for 10 more minutes on low heat.

6. Take a small pan and toast the sesame seeds for 3 minutes on medium heat and keep stirring.

7. Now check the tenderness of the rice and bean mixture—season with pepper and salt.

8. Sprinkle some sesame seeds and drizzle some shoyu or tamari. Garnish with your favorite seasonal herbs. Make this recipe a staple, and try to consume it at least once a week to be proactive.

Indian Mixed Fruit Chat

This rich fruit chat bowl marries all the six tastes of Ayurveda and a blend of Ayurvedic spices. This bowl has fruits like apples, papaya, and banana for the sweet flavor. On the other hand, the pineapple and grapes add the citrus flavor. The Indian gooseberry alone has bitter, sour, and astringent flavors. The fresh Water filled cucumbers, adding crunch to this salad. The sweet dates syrup and tangy tamarind paste give this salad the Indian spin.

The refreshing, lime-like flavor of coriander gives this salad a pungent flavor. This salad was part of our Diwali celebrations in India. I made a large bowl of this salad. And kids picked their favorite fruits from this salad and added more dates syrup on top and enjoyed. You can substitute dates syrup with maple syrup and tamarind paste with lime juice. The cumin powder in this aids in easy digestion and the absorption of nutrients. Enjoy this salad with Indian rose lassi.

Ingredients:

1 cup of chopped papaya cubes

1 cup of chopped apple cubes

3/4 cup of chopped pineapple cubes

1 cup of sliced bananas

1/2 cup of black grapes cut into halves.

1/4 cup of Indian gooseberry

1/2 cup of sliced cucumbers

1 tablespoon green chutney

1 tablespoon finely chopped fresh coriander leaves

1/2 tablespoon of dates syrup

Pinch of turmeric

1/2 tablespoon tamarind paste

1/4 teaspoon black salt

1/2 teaspoon roasted cumin powder

1/4 teaspoon chili powder

1 teaspoon Indian chat masala

Salt to taste

Preparation:

Take a large bowl and add the cubes of papaya, apple, pineapples, black grapes, and Indian gooseberry. Now add in the dates syrup, tamarind paste, chili powder, turmeric, salt, chat masala, and cumin powder. Toss them well and now add in the cucumbers, bananas, and finely chopped coriander leaves and toss them well. Serve them immediately.

Recipes for Hormonal Imbalance

First, what are hormones? Hormones are the chemical messengers that work on sending signals throughout our body, thus affecting the body's functioning in all aspects. The balance of our Hormones affects growth, overall body development, heart rate, metabolism, energy levels, appetite, sleep, sex drive, reproduction, and whatnot.

Due to their impact on various functions of the body, the reason for imbalance may have a wide range of effects. Approximately 80% of women at least once in their lifetime suffer from hormonal imbalance. Symptoms include unexplained sudden weight gain, feeling anxious and depressed, fatigue, mood swings, PMS, insomnia, sweating, low libido, belly fat, loss of muscle mass, digestive issues, poor sleep, foggy memory.

Whereas, in men, low sex drive, infertile sperm, erectile

dysfunction, enlarged breasts, and breast milk production, poor concentration. We need lifestyle changes to keep them in balance. People who are overweight are more prone to imbalance in hormones. The smaller the waistline, it's easy to keep hormones in balance. Secondly, and most importantly, manage your stress. It's impossible to be stress-free, but the way we perceive it and respond to it can be changed. Try yoga, pranayama, and meditation, along with Ayurvedic eating habits. Our kitchen and food are the greatest medicine. These recipes here contain superfoods that help with the hormonal imbalance and the symptoms we experience.

Healthy Hot Chocolate and Nutmeg

As we all know that cocoa helps us during PMS. Dark chocolates are our dear friends when our mood swings kick in. All thanks to cocoa, It nourishes our brain, nervous system, heart, and bones to keep our mood shine bright during bad times. A neurotransmitter called anandamide is known to boost our mood and keeps us calm and happy.

Cinnamon improves insulin sensitivity and allows our

body cells to the effective use of blood glucose into energy rather than being stored as fat. If you are diabetic, you can avoid maple syrup. Coming to nutmeg, This spice is long hailed by Indians and Greeks for its mood-enhancing properties, but it also balances hormones and regulates our menstrual cycles. Nutmeg is popularly called women's Viagra for the same reason. It balances estrogen levels and is known to boosts sex drive. You can also enjoy this scrumptious hot chocolate as a snack time drink.

Ingredients:

2 cups of homemade coconut milk

3 pinches of ground cinnamon

Pinch of turmeric

4 tablespoons of cacao powder

2 shakes of grated nutmeg

1 teaspoon of maple syrup

Preparation:

In a saucepan, boil the coconut milk. Add in the cacao powder, cinnamon, nutmeg powder, turmeric, and finally add maple syrup. Add water if it's too thick. Pour into coffee mugs and enjoy it warm.

According to Ayurveda, to increase the bio-availability of medicinal components of the medicinal herbs and spices, you need to combine them with healthy fats and sweet flavor. So add in the triphala, ashwagandha, ginger, turmeric, or any Ayurvedic herbs. Add them when coconut milk is boiling.

Buckwheat Pancakes

Buckwheat is gaining popularity in America and Europe because it's these golden seeds are gluten-free. But has been popular in Asian cuisine for a long time now. One cup of buckwheat has around 6 grams of protein and 6 grams of fiber. Buckwheat contains d-chiro-inositol, which is used as a supplement for treating metabolic syndrome, PCOS, and gestational diabetes; it also eliminates the excess testosterone and normalizes blood sugar levels.

They mimic the effects of insulin in conditions of insulin resistance.

Whole buckwheat grains are good sources of complex carbohydrates that produce tryptophan, an amino acid that increases the secretion of serotonin, the happy hormone. Carbs can help us with depression and elevate mood. Enjoy these sour pancakes with coconut mint chutney for breakfast.

Ingredients:

1 cup of buckwheat

1/4 cup low fat sour curd

1 teaspoon ginger and chili paste

Pinch of nutmeg powder

2 tablespoon finely chopped coriander

Pinch of turmeric powder

Pinch of asafetida

1/2 cup grated bottle gourd.

4 tablespoon ghee

Salt to taste

Some water

Preparation:

1. In a deep bowl, add the buckwheat, curd, and 2 tablespoons of water and mix well. Cover the lid and keep aside and let it soak for an hour. You can also cover it with a wet muslin cloth.

2. Now, let's blend the mixture to make it a coarse mixture without adding water. Then, into a deep bowl, transfer the coarse buckwheat mixture and add the ginger chili paste, turmeric powder, coriander, asafetida, salt, bottle gourd, and 1 tablespoon water.

3. Mix them well. Keep it aside. Take a nonstick griddle and grease with 1/8 teaspoon ghee. Pour a large spoon of the batter and spread it in a circular motion like we spread dosa batter. Add some ghee and cook till it turns brown on both sides. Serve warm with coconut mint chutney.

Barley Kitchari

Kitchari is an Ayurvedic staple dish usually made of green grams. Barley is rich in soluble fiber known as beta-glucan. Soluble fiber like beta-glucan forms a gel-like substance in our gut, slow down the digestion process and nutrient absorption. This, in turn, will suppress the cravings, hunger and promotes fullness. Eventually, it leads to weight loss over time. Beta-glucans are the most effective form of fiber to suppress hunger and food intake. Selenium is a mineral that plays a major role in the metabolism of thyroid hormones. Moreover, this soluble fiber targets stubborn belly fat that is mainly due to metabolic disease. Barley is rich in selenium, which is an essential mineral that plays major functions with thyroid hormone metabolism. I have replaced rice with barley so that you can enjoy the benefits of this extremely healthy grain barley.

Ingredients:

1/2 cup barley

1 cup split yellow gram

Salt to taste

2 teaspoon ghee

1/4 teaspoon asafetida

1/2 tablespoon cumin seeds

1/4 teaspoon turmeric powder

1 teaspoon finely chopped green chilies

1 teaspoon finely chopped coriander

Preparation:

1. Soak the barley for 30 minutes and drain them.

2. Heat the cooker and add the ghee and cumin seeds. Let the cumin seeds crack.

3. Add the turmeric powder, asafetida, and sauté them for 10 seconds over medium flame.

4. Add in the green chilies and sauté for few more seconds over medium flame.

5. Finally, add the barley, split yellow gram, 4 cups of water, and salt. Mix them well and cook for 30 minutes. And allow steam to escape before you open the lid.

6. Add the chopped coriander and serve it hot. You can add any manner of vegetable to this barley kitchari.

Red Millet Sesame Khakhra

Red millets are called ragi in India, and it's cooked in hundreds of ways. Ragi, aka finger millet, is rich in proteins, vitamin A, B, essential amino acids, fiber, phosphorous. Ragi is popular for its calcium and iron-rich profile and is no parallel among any cereals. In India, it's a popular grain for all ages, from children, pregnant and lactating mothers to old age for the same reason.

I grew up drinking ragi malt every morning, and ragi dosa for breakfast, and ragi cookies, which are amazing, and ragi balls for dinner. It's great for obese and diabetics; the fiber content lowers that bad cholesterol and normalizes the blood sugars, and helps in losing weight. Ragi is an excellent source to improve blood production. You can binge on these guilt-free sesame khakhras.

Ingredients:

1/2 cup whole wheat flour

1/2 cup of red millet flour

2 tablespoon roasted sesame seeds

1/2 teaspoon chili powder

1/4 teaspoon turmeric powder

2 1/4 teaspoon olive oil for kneading the dough and cooking the khakhras.

Salt to taste

1 cup of warm water

Some whole wheat flour for rolling the khakhras.

4 teaspoons of ghee

Preparation:

1. In a deep bowl, add the wheat flour, red millet flour, chili powder, turmeric powder, salt, and warm water and mix them well and knead into a firm dough. Let it rest for 10 minutes. You can cover the dough with a muslin cloth.

2. Add the 1/4 teaspoon of olive oil and divide them into 8 equal portions. Take each portion and roll out with a rolling pin into thin circles. Use some wheat flour for

rolling the khakhras.

3. Heat a non-stick griddle and cook all the khakras on low flame. Use 1/4 teaspoon of ghee and roast them till pink on both sides. Now, continue the cooking of the khakhras on low heat, press the khakhras with the folded muslin cloth. Do this till they turn brown and crispy on both sides.

Serve them immediately, or you can store them in an airtight container.

Kashmiri Khawa Tea

According to Kashmiri folklore, Khawa is a type of green tea that cleanses the digestive system and boosts our metabolism. It is a staple tea in Kashmiri households. It is usually served after lunch; it not only improves digestion but also burns stubborn fat like green tea; weight watchers should get their hands on this tea. It is rich in antioxidants.

Ingredients:

1 teaspoon Kashmiri green tea

1 teaspoon cinnamon powder

3 cups of water

Few saffron strands

1 clove

Half teaspoon dried rose petals

1 crushed cardamom

2 teaspoon slivered almonds

1 teaspoon honey

Preparation:

1. In a pan, boil the water. Add the cinnamon powder, saffron, cloves, cardamom, and dried rose petals into the boiling water and simmer for 2-3 minutes.

2. Now, turn off the heat and add the green tea leaves into the water. Let the khawa and tea steep for one minute.

3. Strain the khawa into cups and add the almond slivers and a few strands of saffron. Sweeten with honey and serve hot.

Kokum Sharbat

Ever heard of the place Goa? Goa is a popular tourist place among foreigners. Kokum is native to goa, and this fruit is commonly used in Goan cuisine. This fruit has a mild sour taste used as a substitute for tamarind. Kokum sharbat is a popular summer drink in India. Kokum sharbat has antioxidants and anti-inflammatory properties. Kokum works best with PCOD and thyroid for symptoms like bloating and headaches. Kokum helps in weight loss; the hydroxy acetic acid present in kokum juice works on lowering the conversion of carbohydrates into fat. It regenerates the fat metabolism. This deep purplish drink reduces body heat. Kokum juice is a natural substitute for those carbonated drinks. Enjoy this drink with your kids during hot summer days.

Ingredients:

1 cup kokum

2 cup of water

1 cup of jaggery

1 teaspoon cumin seeds powder

Pinch of citric acid

3/4 teaspoon black salt

Preparation:

1. In a microwave-safe bowl, add kokum and 1 cup of water and microwave on high for a minute and set aside for 10 minutes.

2. Now drain the mixture of kokum water and set aside the water and kokum.

3. In a blender, combine a half cup of drained kokum water and kokum and blend them to make a smooth paste. Keep it aside.

4. Combine a half cup of water and jaggery powder in a microwave-safe bowl and microwave for 8 minutes on high. Stir frequently after 4 minutes.

5. Add the prepared kokum paste and mix well. Strain it with the help of a sieve and set the kokum sugar mixture, and discard the remains of kokum.

6. Now, to this kokum sugar mixture, let's add the cumin powder, citric acid, and black salt.

7. To serve, add two tablespoons of the kokum mixture into 1/2 cup water from an earthen pot. Store this in an airtight jar and refrigerate.

Healthy Heart Recipes

One in three Americans suffers from heart diseases. Heart disease is the leading cause of death in America. There is one death occurring every 36 seconds from cardiovascular diseases—causes such as physical inactivity, unhealthy dietary choices, diabetes, alcohol abuse, overweight, and obesity. Heart issues are no longer old age problems, especially with diabetes, obesity, and lack of physical activity; heart issues have become equally common among young aged and middle-aged people.

We don't want someone in our family to suffer from heart problems in the future. So, try out these recipes that are rich in fatty acids that are great for heart muscles, and low in sodium and rich in potassium, and potent antioxidants to reverse the free radical damage. So the least we could do is eat healthy for a healthy heart and healthy family.

Sweet Potato Hash Browns

Hash browns are a healthy choice of breakfast, but not the ones you buy at McDonald's; these sweet potatoes hash browns are combined with flax and chia seeds that are rich in alpha-linolenic fatty acid that's good for our heart and sweet potatoes are a nutritious choice, due to high potassium levels, intake of potassium-rich foods work on excreting sodium from the body and lower the blood pressure, in turn preventing cardiovascular diseases.

Coming to orange juice, the potential antioxidant, hesperidin, improves the function of blood vessels and lower the risk of heart disease. Orange zest is known to modify the gut microbes and, in turn, prevent atherosclerosis. Enjoy this alone or along with beans and eggs for breakfast.

Ingredients:

1 grated sweet potato

1 teaspoon of chia seeds

Salt for taste

1 tablespoon of ground flaxseed

1 orange

Freshly ground black pepper

1/2 teaspoon of cinnamon powder

1 tablespoon ghee

1/2 teaspoon of cardamom powder

1/2 teaspoon of clove powder

1 tablespoon of coconut oil

Preparation:

1. In a large bowl filled with cold water, add the grated sweet potato and pinch of salt. Let it soak for an hour. Drain it and pat dry on a kitchen towel.

2. Meanwhile, make orange juice of 1/4 cup and grate the peel to make zest.

3. Take a medium bowl, add the grated sweet potato, flaxseed, and chia seed powder, orange juice, and zest, and spices. Now sprinkle some salt and pepper. Let it sit for 10 minutes.

4. In a skillet, melt 1 tablespoon of coconut oil over medium heat. Add in the sweet potato mixture.

5. Now, use the back of the spoon to spread the mixture evenly on the skillet—cook for 10 minutes without

covering the pot.

6. Now cover it and cook for 10 more minutes. To cook on the other side, uncover the pan, now hold the plate on the hash and flip it over to turn the hash on the plate, now slide back the hash from the plate into the pan—cook without covering for 10 minutes on medium heat.

7. Meanwhile, in a saucepan, melt the ghee. When the hash browns are cooked, serve them on a plate and drizzle the ghee, and season with a pinch of black pepper or salt as needed.

Brussel Sprouts Soup

Brussel sprouts are not just cute; they are healthy veggies for people who want to keep their heart healthy, normalize their blood sugars, and lose weight. For people who don't consume fish, it becomes extremely difficult to meet the daily value of these fatty acids. But Brussel sprouts are a savior for you. Brussel sprouts have a high amount of ALA omega 3 fatty acids in them.135 mg of fatty acids per 78 gram of cooked Brussels. The exclusive antioxidant "kaempferol" that is known for promoting heart health and reduce cancer growth is found in this cutie. Cleanse your heart vessels and nourish them with this creamy ayurvedic brussels sprout soup.

Ingredients:

2 cups of trimmed Brussels sprouts

1 diced onion

2 diced celery stalks

1 diced carrot

1/2 head of cauliflower

1 bunch of chopped parsley

1 teaspoon of curry leaves powder

2 teaspoon of coconut oil

2 minced garlic cloves

2 teaspoon of grated ginger

1/2 teaspoon of turmeric powder

1/4 teaspoon of cayenne pepper

1/2 cup full-fat homemade coconut milk

3 cups of vegetable broth (low sodium)

1/2 teaspoon of pink Himalayan salt

Pinch of asafetida

2 tablespoon of lemon juice

Freshly crushed black pepper

2 teaspoon of hemp hearts

Toasted pine nuts

Preparation:

1. Cut the brussels sprouts into halves. Chop the cauliflower head into a cup of florets.

2. In a soup pot, add in the onion, carrot, garlic, celery, and spices. Drizzle some water and water fry for 5-7 minutes on medium heat while constantly stirring.

3. Add the vegetable broth and coconut milk, boil them over medium heat. Now, on low heat, cook for 15 minutes. Then, add the cauliflower florets and Brussels sprouts and cook for 5 minutes on low heat.

4. Take a blender and add the soup and lime juice, parsley, hemp hearts and blend until you achieve creamy liquid. Add the seasonings, salt, and pepper.

5. Divide into equal serving bowls and garnish with pine nuts. Serve warm.

Tapioca Apricot Pudding

Whenever I think of apricots, I go back to the days of my childhood in Hyderabad, where qurbani ka meetha was served at almost every Hyderabadi wedding. In this dish, we are adding tapioca along with apricots. Apricots are rich in fiber, keeps good cholesterol in, and flushes out bad cholesterol. And potassium in it takes care of heart muscles. Tapioca has zero saturated fat making it a healthy choice for people keeping a check on their cholesterol. Tapioca being low in sodium makes it a great option for people with hypertension.

Ingredients:

½ cup of tapioca pearls

1¾ cups water

1 teaspoon of ghee

¼ teaspoon ground ginger

½ teaspoon of ground cinnamon

Pinch salt

1 cup of plain yogurt

2 tablespoons of Makuna honey

11 dried roughly chopped apricots

½ teaspoon of lemon zest

Preparation:

1. In a small saucepan, boil 1 1/2 cups of water. Add the tapioca pearls. Bring them to a boil in low heat. Now let the tapioca simmer for about 10 minutes. By now, pearls should be dissolved, and tapioca should be creamy.

2. Heat a saucepan and melt the ghee. Add the ground cinnamon, salt, ginger, and sauté for a minute. Add in the apricots and mix well to coat the spicy ghee on them.

3. Now, increase the heat to medium and add the 1/4 cup of water. Bring this to a boil.

4. Turn off the heat, remove the pan, and let the mushy apricots cool for 5 minutes.

5. Now, in a blender, transfer the apricots and juices and pulse to mince them. Add the tapioca into a bowl. Swirl in the apricot mixture and yoghurt. Drizzle some honey and sprinkle some lemon zest. Enjoy!

Blueberry Oatmeal

Blueberries are wildly popular for their impressive antioxidants called anthocyanins, which are responsible for most of the health benefits berries offer. Consuming blueberries reduces bad cholesterol, LDL. It's proven that people who consumed fruits rich in anthocyanins like blueberries had a healthy heart. Coming to oats, the beta-glucan fiber in oats is great for reducing the LDL and total body's cholesterol. Try to incorporate this breakfast at least twice a week to reap the hearty benefits.

Ingredients:

1 cup of fresh blueberries

1 tablespoon honey

2 tablespoon water

1/4 teaspoon vanilla essence

5 sliced almonds

2 whole walnuts

1 cup dried, cooked oats

1 tablespoon ghee

Pinch of salt

1/2 teaspoon cornstarch

Preparation:

1. In a saucepan, add blueberries, honey, vanilla essence, water, pinch of salt, and cook over medium heat for five minutes. Mix well and add the cornstarch and mix again.

2. Bring this to a boil, then let it cook in low heat until it's thickened for about 5 minutes.

3. Serve this on top of the oatmeal and add melted ghee on top.

4. Finally, add the sliced almonds and 2 whole walnuts. You can top it with any of your favorite nuts and raisins. The world is your oyster!

Avocado Mash

An avocado a day keeps the cardiologist away! This fruit, you read it right, avocado is a fruit. This fruit is a great friend of your heart. Our heart loves avocado. The good fats keep your heart happy. Avocado is rich in fiber and phytosterol, which reduces bad cholesterol. So, let your taste buds enjoy this avocado mash as much as your heart does.

Ingredients:

1 pitted avocado

2 tablespoons of ghee or olive oil

Salt for taste

Pinch of turmeric

1 tablespoon of fresh lime juice

1 teaspoon freshly ground black pepper

Preparation:

1. Slice the avocado lengthwise to open, then scoop out the flesh into a bowl.

2. Now, mash the avocado in a small bowl. Add the lime juice, turmeric, salt, and pepper and mix them well; finally, add the ghee or olive oil and mix well and serve them on tortillas, burritos, or as a salad dressing.

Old Age Recipes

Old age is a term of declining physical health. The problems old people face are infinite, firstly losing teeth makes them eat less and mostly consume soft food and then comes the digestive problems which are part of their daily life. Well, that doesn't end there, then comes constipation. Every part of our body undergoes degeneration. Most commonly, old people develop neurodegenerative problems like Parkinson's, Alzheimer's, and dementia with age, but chronic problems like diabetes, heart disease, COPD, hypertension, although they are common, can be prevented with healthy dietary habits. Everything becomes a struggle in old age. Dental problems make it difficult to chew and digest food. So, I have some recipes which are light and not only easy to chew and swallow but are super nutritious too.

Fennel Fava Bean Soup

The famous Sicilian Maccu aka Sicilian fava bean fennel soup is a traditional soup from the Sicily Island in Italy. Fava beans are one of the ancient, domesticated beans that are rich in lean protein and fiber from the pods. One of the common problems in old age is Parkinson's disease. Fava beans are rich in levodopa, a compound that our body converts to dopamine. In Parkinson's, the death of dopamine-producing brain cells leads to tremors, motor dysfunction, and difficulty in walking. It is treated with the medicine levodopa, which is naturally available in fava beans. Enjoy this healthy gift from Sicily for dinner.

Ingredients:

2 cups of dried fava beans

1 chopped fennel bulb along with fronds, chopped

4 cups of vegetable broth

2 chopped celery stalks

4 cups of water

1 lemon

2 tablespoons of ghee

1 teaspoon of sea salt

Freshly crushed black pepper

Extra-virgin olive oil

4 fresh oregano sprigs

Preparation:

1. In a large bowl, soak the beans in cold water for 12 hours. Drain the beans and clean them well.

2. In a large soup pot, add the vegetable broth and water and fava beans and bring them to boil over medium to high heat. Now, reduce the heat to low, cover the lid, and let it cook for an hour.

3. Add the lemon juice and zest—reserve 1 teaspoon of lemon zest for garnishing.

4. Add the fennel bulb, celery with beans, and fennel fronds and cook on low heat for 30 minutes. Drain the fava beans and reserve the broth. Discard the large fronds. Now, transfer the beans into a bowl.

5. In the soup pot, melt the ghee over medium heat.

6. In a blender, add in the beans, fennel, salt, and reserved broth to make a puree. Pour this mixture back into the soup pot.

7. Add in more broth of one cup at a time until you achieve the desired consistency. Now add the lemon juice and the reserved zest.

8. Warm up the soup for another 2 minutes or until very hot. Taste it and add the salt and pepper. Drizzle some olive oil and garnish with a sprig of oregano and lemon zest.

Mixed Vegetable Puree

This mixed vegetable and spice rich soup is quick and easy to make. The prep is to chop the vegetables quickly and roughly. We will blend them to make a puree. You can add any manner of seasonal vegetables like beets, turnips, daikon radishes, fresh peas, cauliflower, carrots, and asparagus. Kombu, an edible seaweed that is a staple among Japanese cuisine, has been linked to promoting health and longevity. Kombu is a nutrition powerhouse, with antioxidants and immunity boosters. This thick and creamy puree is super nutritious and tasty to have in cold winters. You can top this puree with peanuts for a crunchy bite.

Ingredients:

2 cups of seasonal vegetables (roughly chopped)

1 cup of vegetable broth

Pinch of ground ginger

Pinch of ground cinnamon

Pinch of ground cloves

Pinch of turmeric

Pinch of ground fenugreek

1-inch of strip kombu

1 cup of chopped mixed leafy greens like spinach, chard, collards, kale, dandelion leaves

Salt to taste

Freshly crushed black pepper

Sprig of rosemary

Preparation:

1. In a soup pot, add the vegetables, kombu, ground ginger, cinnamon, cloves, turmeric, fenugreek, and bring it to a boil. Then simmer over medium heat for 10 minutes.

2. Add in the chopped leafy greens and cook for 2 more minutes.

3. In a blender, blend the vegetables into a puree. Add salt and pepper, garnish with rosemary, and serve hot.

Curd Rice

Being south Indian, I grew up eating this every day. This is a simple dish made of basic ingredients like curd, rice and topped with south Indian tempering. This curd rice is easy to chew and digest for senior citizens. In India, it's eaten along with tangy pickles. It cools down our tummy and makes digestion easy; it also promotes stronger immunity, reduces your blood pressure issues, and enhances your bone health. Actually, in India, people of all ages and all walks of life eat curd rice at least once a day. Especially older people prefer to consume this healthy dish.

Ingredients:

1/2 cup of boiled brown rice

1 cup fresh homemade curd

1 teaspoon sesame oil

1/2 teaspoon mustard seeds

1/2 teaspoon cumin seeds

8 cashews

1 red chili

1 green chili

5-7 curry leaves

1/2 teaspoon grated ginger

Preparation:

1. In a large bowl, add the boiled rice and add 1 cup of homemade curd. Mix them thoroughly.

2. Now, in a pan, heat 1 tsp of sesame oil and add mustard, cashews, cumin, and red chili. Sauté them.

3. Now, add in the green chilies, ginger, and curry leaves. Turn off the heat and pour this tempering into the curd and rice mixture. Stir it well and serve it.

Pesarattu

Oh yeah, I know, it's a bit hard to pronounce it. But this recipe from Andra, a south Indian state, is a famous breakfast and is usually combined with upma and coconut chutney. Pesarattu is a dish made from soaked green gram, which is super nutritious. It is rich in protein and also helps in better digestion. Green grams are a highly nutritious legume, which also is a very good energy source. Oh, by the way, did I tell you that Pesarattu tastes stupendously tasty? Well, here's how to cook this dish.

Ingredients:

1 cup green gram

2 tablespoon chickpeas

1 cup of water

1 tablespoon rice flour

1 teaspoon salt

7 teaspoons of coconut oil

1 chopped onion

1-inch ginger

1 green chili

Preparation:

1. Take a large mixing bowl and use it to soak the green gram and chickpeas. Make sure that both these ingredients are soaked for 4 to 8 hours. Drain the water off and blend it to get a smooth batter. If needed, add some water.

2. Then, it's time to add some rice flour to make it extra crispy. Add 1 teaspoon of salt.

3. Take a pan, heat it for a couple of minutes, and pour some cooking oil on it. Then, let it heat for a couple more minutes. Then, pour a ladleful of batter on it and spread it properly like how you do it with your pancakes.

4. Now add green chilies and onions. Gently press it so that the onion and chili pieces stick to the batter.

5. Finally, flip it and let it cook for 2-3 minutes before turning off the stove. You can serve it with ketchup, sauce, or stew.

Blueberry Muffin Smoothie

Who doesn't love blueberries? Those sweet and sour fruits are made into a smoothie, which is such a treat for your tongue. These tiny and cute fruits are low in calories yet very rich in nutrients. They're very high in vitamin C, K, manganese, and fiber. It's a very good digestive agent, especially for senior citizens. Moreover, they're also rich in antioxidants, which help in cleansing your whole body. These fruits also aid in better memory, preventing heart diseases, and also lower your blood pressure. This blueberry muffin smoothie contains not only these fruits but also cashews, almonds, and butter as protein sources, which is highly essential for senior citizens.

ingredients:

1 cup of fresh blueberries

1/2 cup of yogurt

1/4 cup of almond milk

1/4 cup of oats

1/4 teaspoon vanilla extract

Pinch of salt

1 teaspoon honey

5-6 cashews

5-6 almonds

Preparation:

Take all the ingredients and add them to a blender. Pulse it until it becomes smooth. You can add milk whenever needed to thin the smoothie out. Consider adding a protein powder instead of cashews and almonds, if you prefer it that way.

Before serving, garnish the smoothie with a few extra

blueberries.

Broccoli Almond Soup

Broccoli is already considered a superfood, especially for the nutrition and fitness experts. Actually, it has become quite a fad to eat it in recent times. However, you may have seen only the gym-goers eating it. Well, broccoli is a very underrated food for senior citizens, and a soup with broccoli as the main ingredient not only offers a lot of energy but also very easy to digest. Along with that, it also helps in reducing excess cholesterol levels, inflammation. Broccoli comes with rich amounts of zinc, magnesium, and phosphorous. It's also rich in fiber, which makes it good digestive food. Coming to almonds, they are rich in proteins, nutrients and are an energy booster.

Ingredients:

2 cups of broccoli florets

1 sliced onion

4 garlic cloves

1 cup of milk

1/4 cup of almonds

A pinch of salt

1 black peppercorn

1 teaspoon olive oil

Preparation:

1. Take a bowl of water and heat it for 5 minutes. Then, soak the almonds in that bowl of hot water for approximately 10 minutes. After that, peel the skin of almonds and set them aside.

2. Now, take a pan, keep it on medium-heat settings, and heat the olive oil in it. After a minute, add onions and garlic. Sauté it till the onions become soft.

3. Now, add in the broccoli florets and sauté it for a couple of minutes. Then, sprinkle the salt before covering the

pan. For 3 to 4 minutes, steam cooks it. Then, turn down the heat and let the mixture cool.

4. Take a blender and add soaked almonds, broccoli mixture, and milk and blend it till it becomes a smooth puree. After blending it, pour the soup onto a saucepan and cook it for a minute. Use black pepper to garnish and serve it hot.

Kiwi Cranberry Juice

The pale green fruit that seems to grab everyone's attention these days has long been considered as one of the most nutritious fruit. It's rich in vitamin C and also comes with good amounts of fiber, aiding in good digestion. Also, Kiwi fruit is a very good antioxidant, making a valuable body cleansing agent. Along with such healthy properties, it's also known to boost our immune system. Since older people suffer from several heart-related health issues, they must consider eating kiwi fruit, as it can reduce the chances of a stroke and other heart diseases. Coming to cranberries, cranberries are hailed for preventing and treating urinary tract infections. Oh btw, cranberries will make us poop! Yes, they are excellent laxatives and prevent constipation in older people.

Ingredients:

2 kiwi fruits

500 ml cranberry juice

2 teaspoon grated ginger

Few fresh mint leaves

Preparation:

Take a blender and use it to blend scooped kiwi fruits and grated ginger. After blending it, add in the cranberry juice and blend it again till it becomes smooth. Pour the smoothed mixture into glasses and garnish it with mint leaves before serving.

Final Words

Although I am a dentist, I found Ayurveda fascinating and therapeutic because it has helped me with my illness. Yes, I suffered from PCOD and had tried all allopathic treatments and dealt with the side effects of these medicines. I had given up on the allopathic way of treatment.

That's when my grandmother told me that pills alone won't help me, and I need to make changes in the way I was living. With my dietary habits, my dosha imbalance, she said to try the Ayurvedic lifestyle for a year and see if it works for you. With no hope of getting the cure and utmost despair, I still went on to try Ayurveda, and to my surprise, I started seeing the results and change in my hormones, and my stubborn bodyweight started coming down my cycles got regular.

It just felt like all-stars were aligned, all my symptoms showed to decline, and I got back on track with my life. All thanks to my grandmother, now I could go back to school, whereas earlier I was getting my blood transfusions and seeking help from multiple doctors. Now I can play with my friends, but earlier I used to watch my friends play.

Well, I would like to give you some facts and wisdom of ancient Ayurveda, which are time and tested. Here are some things my grandmother told me when asked for simple things that I can include in our life. And I want to pass her wisdom to you all through this book.

Ancient Indians stored ghee in large vessels to pass it to future generations because ghee is extremely healthy and was considered as a cure to disorders of the nervous system. Ayurveda is not a vegetarian philosophy, and you don't have to live like an herbivore to live Ayurvedic life. For example, Ayurveda used liver meat to treat marasmus since it is highly nutritious, and marasmus is due to malnutrition. This 5000-year-old ancient science knew about iron deficiency anemia way before the invention of the microscope.

Ayurveda focused on oral hygiene, and my grandparents followed the morning rituals by Ayurveda. They did tongue scraping and oil pulling to remove toxins from our mouths. They used copper tongue scraper; copper has antibacterial properties and scrapes away debris and bacteria from the tongue. They used sesame oil for oil pulling. Oil pulling is called Kavala in Ayurveda. This Ayurvedic dental technique works similar to mouth wash. It involves swishing little oil in our mouth on an empty stomach for a few minutes and spitting it off.

Ayurveda recommends the usage of a cooper utensil to purify water. Ayurveda recommends using dinnerware made of copper. Copper has antibacterial effects, and bacteria cannot survive on copper. Copper can prevent waterborne diseases, as well. Ayurveda suggests the usage of clay pots to cool the water during summers, which is still practiced in many parts of India.

The above-mentioned tips can be followed easily even today, and I have been practicing them in my life too. Try to incorporate these simple things into your daily life. Some Ayurvedic kitchen staples like turmeric, fenugreek, curry leaves, ghee, asafetida, coriander, black pepper, garlic, and ginger is a must-have if you are eating Ayurvedic way.

I thoroughly enjoyed writing these recipes, which I have been eating all my life. I have enjoyed the process of curating recipes for certain health issues. I hope you will try them and get benefit from them. I hope this book adds value to your life. Finally, I thank you- NAMASTE, from the bottom of my heart for trusting in me and getting your hands on this book.

www.ingramcontent.com/pod-product-compliance
Lightning Source LLC
Chambersburg PA
CBHW070325220526
45467CB00001B/35